Healthy Eating, Exercise, and Sleep

Author:	Jacob Nelson, B.S. Exercise Science, NASM, ACSM-EP
Editor:	Mary Dieterich
Proofreaders:	Margaret Brown and Alexis Fey

COPYRIGHT © 2024 Mark Twain Media, Inc.

ISBN 978-1-62223-893-4

Printing No. CD-405086

Mark Twain Media, Inc., Publishers
Distributed by Carson Dellosa Education

Table of Contents

Table of Contents (cont.)

Introduction

Healthy Eating, Exercise, and Sleep is designed to teach students about nutrition, healthy food choices, healthy exercise types, sleep, and recovery, setting the foundation to building healthy lifestyle habits that will allow students to continue living long and healthy lives. Education on living a health-oriented lifestyle is just the beginning. Taking the lessons and applying them to build lifelong habits will ensure healthy aging and a better relationship with food and exercise. With childhood obesity on the rise, education on the basic principles of nutrition and exercise early on in life is the key to helping the nation's most vulnerable population start off life on the right foot—fit spiritually, mentally, and physically.

This book is organized into different chapters that focus on the basic principles of nutrition, understanding how to read a food label, understanding how your body produces and burns off energy, the different types of exercise for different purposes, and how eating healthy, exercise, and better sleep can help students prevent disease, focusing on prevention as being the best medicine.

The goal of this book is to empower students to build healthy exercise habits and healthier relationships with food. Key terms will be defined as the book goes on. All of the key terms will help to familiarize students with relevant nutritional and exercise information and provide a baseline understanding of food and exercise. With so many "fad diets" promising to solve all the world's problems, it is important to lay a solid foundation of sound science-backed understanding so students can practice critical thinking as adults when making nutritional and exercise decisions.

The activities within this book have been designed to help students and maybe even teachers take control of their lives and build healthier long-lasting habits that will improve their quality of life for years to come. Each individual is a blank slate in middle school and high school. The habits they build and develop in their teenage years can potentially stick with them for the remainder of their lives. This is why it is so important to educate students on healthy choices and help them build a foundation of habits that will ensure their health and wellness down

the road. The mind follows the body, so taking care of the body will help them take care of their minds and lead to an overall higher quality of life.

Nutrition at a Glance

Chapter 1: Basics of Nutrition

Nutrition Overview

Nutrition can be defined as the study of how food affects the human body and its processes. This includes digesting and how the body uses the nutrients after digesting. It is understanding the different components of food, such as calories, carbohydrates, proteins, fats, vitamins, minerals, and fiber and how they impact the body's overall health and well-being. Proper nutrition is crucial for growing children, maintaining overall physical health, maintaining mental health, and preventing chronic diseases. The purpose of this chapter is to provide information on understanding calories, protein, fat, carbohydrates, minerals, vitamins, and fiber and how they are used in the body.

Calories

Calories are a unit of measurement that tells us how much energy is in the food we eat. We then use that energy and burn calories via living and exercise. This is one of the most important things to understand throughout this chapter—calories just tell us how much energy we get out of a particular food. With this being said, there are no "bad" calories and there are no "good" calories. There are more satisfying and higher nutrient-dense foods, a subject we will expand on later, but there are no "good" or "bad" calories.

An easy way to think about calories is to think about gasoline and your car. If your car gets 30 miles per gallon of gasoline, then 1 gallon of gasoline will allow you to travel 30 miles in your vehicle. Calories are like gasoline and you are like the car. If walking 1 mile burns 100 calories and one apple has 100 calories in it, then eating that one apple will sufficiently fuel that entire mile walk. If you were walking 1 mile and you ate one big piece of cake that had 300 calories in it, you would burn the 100 calories from the walk but still have 200 calories left over. These calories would then be stored for your body to use at a later time—either in the form of **glycogen** (your body's stored sugar located inside the liver and muscle) or **fat** (your body's preferred stored energy). This isn't necessarily a bad thing as long as you continue to be active to burn off the excess calories, but if you live a sedentary lifestyle, then continuing to eat high-calorie (energy) foods and

not burn them off, your body will likely store a lot of the excess calories as fat. That is usually where people get into trouble.

Now, if you were to walk 3 miles, then the apple would not be enough fuel to fuel that entire walk so your body would have to either burn off some of its glycogen stores or its fat stores. If you ate the piece of cake, then your body would have enough calories for the entire walk, and you wouldn't store any of the calories as glycogen or fat. So, was the cake a bad choice? Well, as you can see, it depends on what you're doing. Like most things in life, it is not as black and white as one might think. If your goal is to lose body fat, then you would be better off only eating the apple and going on your 3-mile walk. If your goal is to stay the same body weight, then you could eat the cake and come out even after the 3-mile walk. Calories are just energy. How they are used and stored is totally up to you and your daily activities. This is where energy balance and keeping a calorie budget will come into play later on in the text.

Chapter 1: Basics of Nutrition (cont.)

Macronutrients

Calories can be further broken down into 3 distinct nutrients called "macronutrients" or in common slang "macros." **Macronutrients** are the core nutrients required by the body to provide energy, support growth, and maintain the body's metabolic functions. The three macronutrients are **protein**, **carbohydrates**, and **fats**.

Protein is the essential macronutrient used by the body to build and repair tissues, produce enzymes, help produce hormones, support immune function, and provide energy when carbohydrates and fat stores are low. Protein is made up of building blocks called **amino acids**. Amino acids can be thought of as the "bricks" making up a "brick house." Some amino acids can be produced on their own by the body but some have to be eaten in food. If a food contains all the amino acids we need, it is known as a **complete protein**. **Protein contains 4 calories per gram.**

Protein is found in a variety of foods such as meat, fish, poultry, eggs, dairy, beans, nuts, seeds, and tofu. Different foods contain different types of amino acids, so it is important to eat a variety of these foods to ensure you're getting all of the different amino acids you need. Your lean body mass and muscle are made up of protein. This is crucial to understand for exercise. The more you exercise, the more protein you will need to repair and build up tissue. Protein also makes up your hair, skin, nails, and the chemicals in your brain responsible for making you happy, satisfied, and focused. Protein is a crucial part of your diet and should not be limited or minimized. A lack of protein during childhood can stunt your growth and impair puberty.

Carbohydrates, or carbs, are an essential macronutrient responsible primarily for energy. Carbohydrates are digested and broken down into **glucose**, which is the body's primary source of fuel. There are two main types of carbohydrates. They can be categorized into **complex carbohydrates** and **simple carbohydrates**. You can think of simple carbohydrates as fast and quick energy and complex carbohydrates as long and steady energy. Eating simple carbohydrates spikes your blood sugar quickly, which can lead to various diseases if excessive. Complex carbohydrates have a much smaller effect on blood sugar spikes, which can decrease the likelihood of diseases like diabetes. **Carbohydrates contain 4 calories per gram.**

Simple carbohydrates are also known as sugars. They are found in fruits, vegetables, and dairy products and are added in a lot of processed foods to make them taste sweeter (like candy). Simple carbohydrates are quickly digested and therefore are useful for fast energy. If you are about to go on a run or have football practice, eating simple carbohydrates would be a good strategy to fuel that workout. If you are going to sit at your desk for a few hours, then you don't really need a ton of "fast energy," so simple carbohydrates would NOT be very beneficial for that activity. Simply put, simple carbohydrates are best used when you're about to do something physically demanding.

Chapter 1: Basics of Nutrition (cont.)

Complex Carbohydrates are known as starches. They are found in grains, legumes, and starchy vegetables like potatoes. Because they are complex, it takes the body longer to break them down to use as energy. This means you'll get slow and steady energy from complex carbohydrates over the course of several hours. A good strategy for complex carbohydrates would be to eat them for breakfast. This will ensure that you have plenty of energy throughout your morning at school or at work. Eating them at lunch would also help you carry on the second half of your school or work day and provide sufficient energy for your activities later on in the day.

Fiber is a type of carbohydrate that your body cannot digest or absorb. Think about fiber as a cleaning nutrient. It helps clean out your gut and keep regular digestion and bowel movements. Fiber also fills your stomach up without many calories, so eating more of it is a good weight maintenance strategy as it will keep you full longer in between meals. Fiber also slows down the digestion of some foods. When digestion is slower, that means you have more long-sustained energy and less blood sugar spikes (think back to complex carbohydrates). Diets high in fiber have been shown to decrease cancer, heart disease, and diabetes. There are two types of fiber, **soluble** and **insoluble fiber**.

Soluble fiber means the fiber dissolves in water (your stomach is full of water). It creates a gel-like substance inside the stomach. It can help lower cholesterol, regulate blood sugar, and is high in satiety, which means it keeps you feeling full for a long time. Foods high in soluble fiber include lentils, fruits, vegetables, and oats.

Insoluble fiber does not dissolve in water, but adds "bulk" to your stool. It helps promote regular bowel movements by preventing constipation. Whole foods are typically very high in fiber. Whole wheat, nuts, seeds, quinoa, vegetables, and brown rice all contain large amounts of fiber. This is why people generally go to the bathroom more often when they eat whole foods—they contain more fiber.

Fats, also known as lipids, are also essential macronutrients for maintaining human health. Fats, like carbohydrates, provide energy for us to use, but they also cushion and protect organs, help regulate body temperature, are involved with the production of hormones, and make up the majority of our brain. There are three types of fats: **saturated, monounsaturated**, and **polyunsaturated**. **Fat contains 9 calories per gram.**

Saturated fats are found in a lot of animal products. They are typically solid at room temperature such as butter, cheese, and fatty meats. Saturated fats are predominantly used for hormone production (testosterone, estrogen, and progesterone), cell membrane function, and absorbing fat-soluble vitamins like A, D, E, and K that influence a lot of functions within the body.

Chapter 1: Basics of Nutrition (cont.)

While saturated fat does a lot of great things for the body, too much can increase the likelihood of disease, so it is important not to overeat.

Monounsaturated and **polyunsaturated fats** from foods such as olive oil, canola/vegetable oil, avocados, nuts, and seeds are typically liquid at room temperature. Similar to saturated fats, they maintain healthy cells in the body and aid in the absorption of fat-soluble vitamins. They can improve healthy cholesterol levels and reduce the risk of heart disease and stroke. Olive oil and fish oil are considered to be two of the healthiest types of fats we can consume, containing large amounts of omega-3 fatty acids.

Micronutrients

Micronutrients are much smaller components found within the food we eat. Micronutrients can be divided up into vitamins and minerals, but also contain compounds such as antioxidants and phytochemicals that have many positive impacts on health and wellbeing.

Vitamins are *organic compounds* essential for normal metabolism and growth throughout the body. **Organic compounds** are derived from living things, plants or animals, either directly or indirectly. Organic compounds contain carbon atoms. Vitamins are classified into two groups: **water soluble** and **fat soluble**. *Soluble* just means what the vitamin can be dissolved and stored in, so something **water soluble** means it can be absorbed in water. This means if you take too much of it, you can urinate it out so it's very hard to overdose. **Fat soluble** means it dissolves into fat, so the excess of those vitamins is stored in our fat tissue. Since fat-soluble vitamins are saved inside our fat tissue and we can't urinate them out, it's possible to consume too much of them and reach toxic levels—although it's very hard to do.

Minerals are *inorganic compounds* that are also essential for many functions throughout the body. **Inorganic compounds** do not contain carbon and do not come from living sources. Minerals are further classified into **major minerals**, like calcium, magnesium, sodium, and potassium, and **trace minerals**, such as iron, zinc, and copper.

Antioxidants and **phytochemicals** are compounds found in many plant foods that have a lot of potential to reduce chronic diseases such as cancer and heart disease. This is why it's so important to eat your vegetables!

Chapter 1: Basics of Nutrition (cont.)

Daily Nutritional Goals

The following chart lists the amounts or percentages of the calories consumed of macronutrients, minerals, and vitamins that you should aim for each day. These are guidelines to try to follow as an average each day.

Macronutrients, Minerals, & Vitamins		Age/Sex Groups			
		F 9-13	F 14-18	M 9-13	M 14-18
Calorie Level Assessed		1,600	1,800	1,800	2,200
	Source of Goal				
Macronutrients					
Protein (% kcal)	AMDR	10-30	10-30	10-30	10-30
Protein (g)	RDA	34	46	34	52
Carbohydrate (% kcal)	AMDR	45-65	45-65	45-65	45-65
Carbohydrate (g)	RDA	130	130	130	130
Fiber (g)	14 g/1,000 kcal	22	25	25	31
Added Sugars (% kcal)	DGA	<10	<10	<10	<10
Total lipid (% kcal)	AMDR	25-35	25-35	25-35	25-35
Saturated Fatty Acids (% kcal)	DGA	<10	<10	<10	<10
18:2 Linoleic Acid (g)	AI	10	11	12	16
18:3 Linoleic Acid (g)	AI	1.0	1.1	1.2	1.6
Minerals					
Calcium (mg)	RDA	1,300	1,300	1,300	1,300
Iron (mg)	RDA	8	15	8	11
Magnesium (mg)	RDA	240	360	240	410
Phosphorus (mg)	RDA	1,250	1,250	1,250	1,250
Potassium (mg)	AI	2,300	2,300	2,500	3,000
Sodium (mg)	CDRR	1,800	2,300	1,800	2,300
Zinc (mg)	RDA	8	9	8	11
Vitamins					
Vitamin A (mcg RAE)	RDA	600	700	600	900
Vitamin E (mg AT)	RDA	11	15	11	15
Vitamin D (IU)	RDA	600	600	600	600
Vitamin C (mg)	RDA	45	65	45	75
Thiamin (mg)	RDA	0.9	1.0	0.9	1.2
Riboflavin (mg)	RDA	0.9	1.0	0.9	1.3
Niacin (mg)	RDA	12	14	12	16
Vitamin B-6 (mg)	RDA	1.0	1.2	1.0	1.3
Vitamin B-12 (mcg)	RDA	1.8	2.4	1.8	2.4
Choline (mg)	AI	375	400	375	550
Vitamin K (mcg)	AI	60	75	60	75
Folate (mcg DFE)	RDA	300	400	300	400

Abbreviations:
g = gram
mg = milligram
mcg = microgram
AI = Adequate Intake
CDRR = Chronic Disease Risk Reduction Level
DGA = *Dietary Guidelines for Americans, 2020–2025*
RDA = Recommended Dietary Allowance
AT = alpha-tocopherol
DFE = Dietary Folate Equivalent
IU = International Units
RAE = Retinol Activity Equivalents

Data exerpted from:
"Daily Nutritional Goals, Ages 2 and Older." *Dietary Guidelines for Americans, 2020–2025.* 9th ed. Appendix 1, Table A1–2. pg. 134. Washington, DC: U.S. Departments of Health and Human Services (HHS) and Agriculture (USDA); 2020. Available at <DietaryGuidelines.gov>.

Chapter 1: Basics of Nutrition (cont.)

Nutrient-dense Foods

Nutrient-dense foods just simply mean they have a lot of micronutrients. This is the major difference between **whole foods** and heavily **processed foods**. **Whole foods** you can think about as having pretty close to one ingredient. Chicken, lettuce, blueberries, eggs, almonds, and sweet potatoes can be categorized as whole foods. Whole foods have all of their micronutrients intact and are generally lower in calories. All of these foods contain plenty of vitamins, whereas foods like pizza and ice cream are heavily processed, which usually means many of the vitamins and minerals are taken out of the foods. This creates a problem; ice cream and pizza have a lot of MACRONUTRIENTS but have very few MICRONUTRIENTS. That means they contain many calories but do not have very many vitamins and minerals. If your diet consists of only processed food, you can become malnourished from a vitamin and mineral standpoint, which can stunt your growth, weaken your immune system, weaken your mental health, cause cognitive impairment, and cause anemia. Because you're technically eating enough, or usually too many, calories with processed food, your body will store the excess as fat—so you can be malnourished from a vitamin and mineral standpoint but still be overweight.

Think back to our discussion on an apple versus a piece of cake. Apples contain vitamin C, fiber, potassium, and contain phytonutrients such as quercetin, pectin, and polyphenols that all help protect against diseases. This apple also contains 100 calories. A piece of cake might have 300 calories but it has hardly any of the vitamins and minerals the apple has. This means the apple has a higher nutrient density than the piece of cake, which means the apple is the better choice to make sure you're getting all your nutrients.

Comparing a chicken breast to a slice of pizza, a 6-ounce piece of chicken contains 231 calories, 43 grams of protein, and 5 grams of fat. Chicken also contains sodium, potassium, zinc, B vitamins, choline, and betaine, making it very nutrient dense. With chicken, you get a lot of protein with very few calories, which is great for keeping body fat low and muscle mass high. A slice of pizza, however, will have closer to 300–400 calories, 30–40 grams of carbs, 12–15 grams of protein, 14–20 grams of fat, very little vitamins, and a lot of sodium and saturated fat. Pizza is much higher in calories and much lower in protein, so it's usually not a great choice compared to chicken breast. Now if you are someone who is having trouble GAINING weight or you are someone who exercises a lot, pizza might be a great choice to get extra calories in. You could even opt for a pizza with chicken on it. This would help get the protein and micronutrients up without increasing the fat or calories as much.

Like most things in life, balance is the key. The key to long-term success is making the foods you enjoy healthier. This works a lot better than "never eating pizza again." Things like cauliflower crust, chicken crust, and other low-carb crusts can lower the calorie content and increase the nutrient density of pizza, then picking sensible toppings like supreme pizza or bbq chicken pizza can make it more nutritious too.

Chapter 1: Basics of Nutrition (cont.)

Reading a Food Label

Being able to read a **food label** is as important as being able to balance the money in your bank account. If you can't balance the money in your bank account, how do you know if you have enough money to buy anything at the grocery store? You have to be able to read a food label in order to know what you're putting in your body and if it makes sense for you. This is how you make fully educated decisions on your food. This example is from the CDC, and more information on reading food labels can be found on their website at <https://www.cdc.gov/diabetes/managing/eat-well/food-labels.html>.

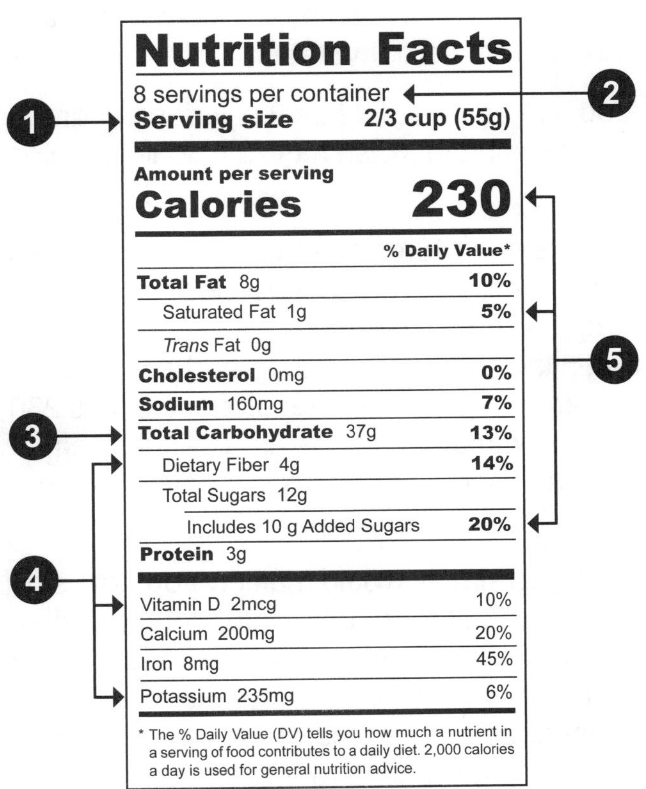

1. Check the **Serving Size** first. This example lists the serving size as 2/3 cup, so all the information below provides information on JUST that serving size.

2. **This package has 8 servings per container.** That means there are **8** 2/3-cup servings within this box of food. For example, if you are just eating 1 serving, this box would feed 8 people because there are 8 servings in the container.

3. **Total Carbohydrate** shows you how many carbs and the types of carbs found in one serving of this food. Above the carbs, you can also see **Total Fat** and the types of fat found within it. Below the carbs, you can see **Protein** and how many grams of protein there are. There is a **% Daily Value** listed beside the macronutrients. This is based on a 2,000-calorie diet, which may or may not be accurate depending on your size and bodily growth demands (going through puberty for instance) or level of exercise, so while these percentages are important, they are highly dependent on the individual.

4. **Choose foods that have high percentages of fiber, vitamins, and minerals**.

5. **Choose foods lower in calories, saturated fat, and added sugars**.

6. The package should also contain an **ingredients list** with items listed from greatest amount to least. A list of known **allergens** should also be given, such as milk, soy, or nuts. Make note of any **additives and preservatives** in the ingredients list. Fresher foods without additives and preservatives are usually better for you.

7. So-called **"expiration dates"** on packages are an indication of when a food will have the best quality, not necessarily when it will "go bad." A **"sell-by date"** tells the grocer when to remove older products from the shelf. A **"best-by date"** indicates the food will taste better if used by this date. Regardless of the date, it is best to use or freeze perishable foods within a few days of purchase. Shelf-stable foods may be used after the "best-by date," but the quality will go down over time.

Chapter 1: Basics of Nutrition (cont.)

Think back to first introducing the macronutrients protein, fat, and carbohydrates. Protein contains 4 calories per gram, carbohydrates contain 4 calories per gram, and fat contains 9 calories per gram. Food labels, as you can see on page 7, are based on grams so this is why it's important to know how many calories per gram each macronutrient has.

This particular food has 3 grams of protein. If you take 3 (grams) and multiply it by 4 (since protein has 4 calories per gram) you get 12. That means this food has 12 calories coming from protein.

This food contains 37 grams of carbohydrates. 37 (grams) multiplied by 4 (since carbs have 4 calories per gram) is 148. That means 148 calories come from carbohydrates.

There are 8 grams of fat within this serving of food. Remember, fat has 9 calories per gram, so we would multiply 8 x 9 and we would come out to 72, meaning this dish has 72 calories coming from fat.

Now, by putting it all together, 12 calories from protein + 148 calories from carbohydrates + 72 calories from fat = 232 total calories. Does that look familiar? That is very close to the 230 calories per serving size. Many food labels and packages are allowed to be "off" by up to 20% on their food labels. They also have rounding rules that allow them to round up and down to the nearest gram. This is why we came out to 232 calories even though the serving size listed it as 230 calories. This is also why it is so important to understand how many calories are in each gram of your macronutrient. Knowing how to calculate your calories based on grams is like balancing your checkbook.

If you plan on eating the entire box of food yourself, you simply would multiply your totals by 8 since there are **8 servings per container**. This would come out to roughly 1,800 total calories, 24 grams of protein, 296 grams of carbohydrates, and 64 grams of carbs. If you were just going to eat half the box by yourself, you would only multiply it by 4, which would come out to 900 total calories, 12 grams of protein, 148 grams of carbohydrates, and 32 grams of fat. So, whenever you're eating something, measure out how many servings you are eating to find the total amount of calories, macronutrients, and micronutrients.

After doing the breakdown, you can see this food is very low in protein, moderate in fat, and high in carbohydrates. Pretend this food shown is macaroni and cheese. It would not be very wise to eat an entire plate of macaroni because you wouldn't get very much protein. However, by eating a variety of food, you can pair up this macaroni with a chicken or turkey breast during your meal. Chicken and turkey are both very high in protein and very low in fat. By eating less macaroni and pairing it with a higher protein main course meal, you are increasing the protein in that meal and making it much more balanced. There are also different kinds of vitamins and minerals in the protein than there are in the macaroni and cheese, so this will help make sure you're not deficient in any one thing.

Chapter 1: Basics of Nutrition (cont.)

You can practice this skill by looking up your favorite foods and calculating how many calories of fat, carbohydrates, and protein are in each serving. Usually you want about 20% of the calories to

come from fat, 30% from protein, and 50% from carbohydrates. This is also dependent on your activity level and your goals. If gaining muscle for sports is your goal, you might want more protein in a particular meal since protein is what builds muscle mass. If you are going on a long-distance race, you might want more carbs in that meal to help fuel your workout. Perspective matters and individual preferences also matter, but generally try to make sure you have a balance between protein, carbs, and fat and that there are high percentages of fiber, vitamins, and minerals in whatever you're eating. Food labels won't always label all the micronutrients, so you can also search online and see how much of each vitamin and mineral your food contains.

Key Notes
- **Nutrition** can be defined as the study of how food affects the human body and its processes.
- **Calories** are a unit of measurement that tells us how much energy is in the food we eat. We then use that energy and burn calories via living and exercise.
- **Macronutrients** are the core nutrients required by the body to provide energy, support growth, and maintain the body's metabolic functions.
  - **Protein** is the essential macronutrient used by the body to build and repair tissues, produce enzymes, help produce hormones, support immune function, and provide energy when carbohydrates and fat stores are low. Protein has 4 calories per gram. Protein is made up of amino acids.
    - **Amino acids** can be thought of as the "bricks" making up a "brick house."
  - **Carbohydrates**, or carbs, are an essential macronutrient responsible primarily for energy. Carbohydrates have 4 calories per gram. Carbohydrates can be broken down into simple carbohydrates or complex carbohydrates. Fiber is also a carbohydrate.
    - **Simple carbohydrates** are also known as sugars. They are found in fruits, vegetables, and dairy products. They are quickly digested and therefore are useful for fast energy.
    - **Complex carbohydrates** are known as starches. They are found in grains, legumes, and starchy vegetables like potatoes. Because they are complex, it takes the body longer to break them down to use as energy, and therefore, they are useful for long-lasting energy.
    - **Fiber** is a type of carbohydrate that your body cannot digest or absorb. Think about fiber as a cleaning nutrient. It helps clean out your gut and keep regular digestion and bowel movements. There are two types of fiber, insoluble and soluble.
      - **Soluble fiber** dissolves in water and creates a gel-like substance inside your stomach.
      - **Insoluble fiber** does not dissolve in water but adds "bulk" to your stool. It helps promote regular bowel movements by preventing constipation.

Chapter 1: Basics of Nutrition (cont.)

- ◆ **Fats**, also known as lipids, are also essential macronutrients for maintaining human health. Fats, like carbohydrates, provide energy for us to use, but they also cushion and protect organs, help regulate body temperature, are involved with the production of hormones, and make up the majority of our brain. There are three types of fats: saturated, monounsaturated, and polyunsaturated. Fat contains 9 calories per gram.
    - ❏ **Saturated fats** are solid at room temperature and are used for hormone production, cell membrane function, and absorbing fat soluble vitamins like A, D, E, and K.
    - ❏ **Monounsaturated** and **polyunsaturated fats** are liquid at room temperature and help promote healthy cholesterol levels, which decrease the likelihood of cardiovascular disease.
- ● **Micronutrients** can be divided up into vitamins and minerals, but also contain compounds such as antioxidants and phytochemicals that have many positive impacts on health and wellbeing.
    - ◆ **Vitamins** are organic compounds essential for normal metabolism and growth throughout the body. They are classified into two groups: water soluble and fat soluble.
    - ◆ **Minerals** are inorganic compounds that are also essential for many bodily functions throughout the body.
    - ◆ **Antioxidants** and **phytochemicals** are compounds found in many plant foods that have a lot of potential to reduce chronic diseases such as cancer and heart disease.
- ● **Daily Nutritional Goals** are guidelines for macronutrients, minerals, and vitamins from *Dietary Guidelines for Americans, 2020–2025*
- ● **Nutrient density** refers to foods high in macronutrients and micronutrients.
- ● **Food labels** are nutrition labels found on the backs of food packages that include standardized nutritional content, ingredients, and other relevant information about the food, including allergies.
    - ◆ **Serving Size**
    - ◆ **Calories**
    - ◆ **Nutrient Information**
    - ◆ **% Daily Value**
    - ◆ **Ingredient List**
    - ◆ **Allergen Information**
    - ◆ **Additives and Preservatives**
    - ◆ **"Expiration Date"**

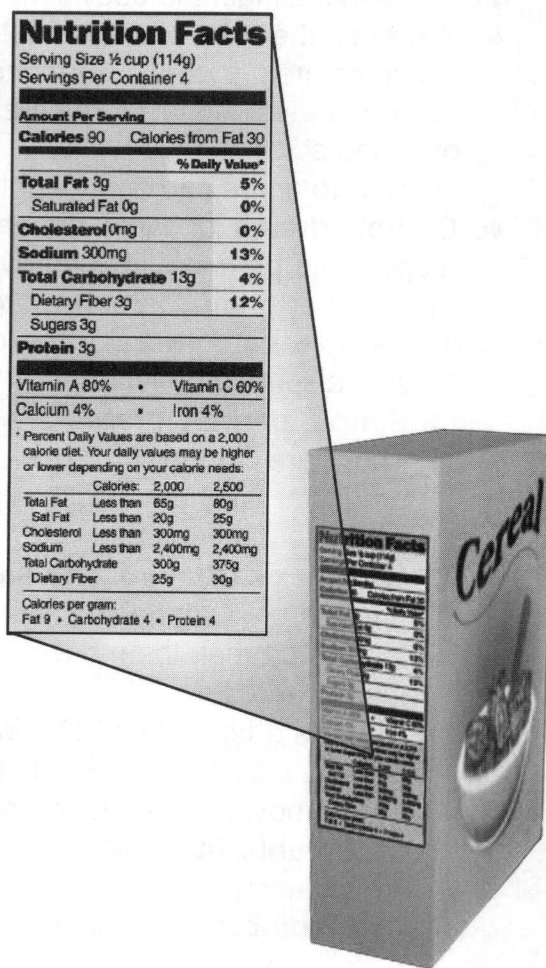

Chapter 1: Basics of Nutrition (cont.)

Activity: What's Really in Your Favorite Food?

Instructions for Students: Bring in your favorite nonperishable food from home still in its original packaging. Find the nutrition label on the packaging. Also bring in disposable plates or containers to separate the food. The teacher may want to provide these.

1. If possible, measure out one serving of the food so you can see how big the serving size actually is.
   a. You may be shocked to see how small a serving size of common goods like peanut butter actually is and how those calories really add up.
2. Break down the package of food into its various serving sizes and separate into piles so you can visually see how many servings each container of food has and how big the servings actually are.
3. Break down the nutrient information: calories, protein, carbohydrates, and fat according to the nutrient label. Ask yourself, does this food have a lot of protein? Is it very carb heavy? Does it have a lot of fat? Does it have a lot of calories?
   a. Break down the % Daily Value per serving. Look for micronutrients and minerals as well. If there aren't many listed, have the students go online to the U. S. Department of Agriculture and look up the food and find more nutritional information on it there.
      i. <https://fdc.nal.usda.gov/>
      ii. Does this food have a lot of the vitamins and minerals you need?
   b. List how many ingredients are in each of the favorite foods. Remember, the fewer the ingredients, the closer the food is to being a whole food, which has more vitamins, minerals, and is less processed. Foods with longer ingredient lists are generally more processed.
   c. Examine the expiration date. Foods that expire quickly are usually fresher and contain less preservatives. Foods that have long expiration dates typically have more preservatives and chemicals that help them last longer. Generally, fresher food is a healthier choice.

The goal of breaking down your favorite foods is to show you how big a serving size really is. Overconsumption is one of the leading causes of obesity in the United States. Children and teens need to learn portion sizes, which starts with learning how big the serving sizes of your favorite foods actually are. This helps you eat in moderation and understand just how many calories you're consuming per meal. More importantly, some of these meals might not contain any protein and may be high in carbohydrates and fat. It is important that the foods you pick are balanced and contain a lot of micronutrients.

Energy Balance: Calories in Versus Calories Out

Chapter 2: Understanding Energy Balance

Energy Balance Overview

Energy Balance refers to the total amount of energy (calories) being consumed and the total amount of energy being used up by the body. Using the car example, if you have to drive 30 miles and your car gets 30 miles per gallon so you put 1 gallon of gasoline in your car, that energy balance is thought to be "neutral" because you are using the exact same amount of energy as you're putting in. If you had to go 35 miles, but you only put 1 gallon of gas in, then that means you would not reach your destination. This can be defined as a negative energy balance because you didn't have enough fuel to get to where you were going. If you only had to go 25 miles, but you still put a whole gallon in, you would have 5 miles left over. This can be defined as being in a positive energy balance because you have more than enough gas to keep going.

Now remember, gasoline is equivalent to calories, and your body is the moving car. The United States Dietary Guidelines say females who are moderately active use 2,000–2,200 calories per day, meanwhile moderately active males use closer to 2,400–2,800 calories per day. Males are typically bigger and have more muscle mass, which means they require more fuel to stay alive. So, in simple terms, if you burn 2,200 calories per day, you would have to eat 2,200 calories per day to stay at the same body weight. This means you would be in a **neutral energy balance**. If you only ate 1,800 calories per day but you burned 2,200 calories per day, you wouldn't be eating enough to maintain your body weight, so you would **lose** weight because you were in a **negative energy balance**. If you were only burning 2,200 calories per day, but you were eating 3,000 calories per day, you would **gain** weight because you were in a **positive energy balance**. One day of eating less or one day of eating more isn't enough to significantly lose or gain weight so you don't have to be exact every single day, but being consistently in a negative energy balance will lead to weight loss and being consistently in a positive energy balance will lead to weight gain.

Components of Energy Balance Metabolism

Metabolism is defined as the chemical processes that occur within a living organism in order to maintain life. From a nutrition standpoint, this includes all the processes by which food and nutrients are broken down to produce energy, repair tissue, and build all the hormones, neurotransmitters, cells, and all of the things that keep us alive. Your metabolism can be thought of as your body burning calories. There are four major components that make up your metabolism: your **basal metabolic rate**, **non-exercise activity thermogenesis**, **thermogenic effect of food**, and **exercise activity thermogenesis**. *Thermogenesis* can be broken down into "heat" for *thermo* and "creation" for *genesis*. When you think of heat, think of burning coal or burning energy. **Thermogenesis** simply means burning energy. By combining these four factors of metabolism, an individual would be able to estimate their **Total Daily Energy Expenditure (TDEE)** to calculate how many calories they need per day based on their own body and activity level.

Chapter 2: Understanding Energy Balance (cont.)

Basal Metabolic Rate (BMR) is the number of calories a person needs per day to continue breathing, circulating blood, maintaining body temperature, and essentially staying alive. BMR can be thought of as how many calories you would burn if you were to lie in bed all day long and not move. BMR makes up close to 70% of the total calories you burn all day long. Your age, sex, height, weight, and body composition influence your BMR. The taller and bigger you are, the more calories you will burn because you have more tissue to keep alive. The smaller you are, the fewer calories you will burn because there's not as

The number of calories a person burns in a day varies even among active people according to their age, sex, weight, and body composition.

many tissues. If you want to increase your BMR and burn more calories by resistance training and building muscle, you will increase your body weight in a healthy way, thus speeding up your metabolism and allowing you to eat more food. This is one of the key factors of people who are thought to have "slow" metabolisms and people who have "fast" metabolisms. Think of athletes versus sedentary adults. Athletes have a lot of muscle mass so they have to eat a lot of food to sustain all that muscle, whereas a person who doesn't work out very much doesn't have a lot of muscle mass to sustain so they don't need to eat as much.

Non-Exercise Activity Thermogenesis (NEAT) refers to the total amount of calories you burn per day doing basic movements like walking, standing, fidgeting, or even typing. NEAT can account for 15–50% of an individual's total energy expenditure, depending on daily activity. If you sit at a desk all day at work, you won't burn very many NEAT calories because sitting down is very easy to do. If you work construction and are walking all day long, you would burn a great deal of calories because you're moving around so much at work. Even people who fidget often can burn a lot of extra calories per day. If you want to increase the number of NEAT calories you burn, take standing and walking breaks throughout the day. Take the stairs instead of the elevator, park farther from the grocery store, or take your animals out for walks frequently. Essentially, live an active lifestyle, and those small habits will increase the number of calories you burn per day.

Thermogenic Effect of Food refers to the calories it takes to digest, absorb, and metabolize the nutrients in food. Yes, it burns calories just to digest calories! Protein has the highest thermogenic effect of food. Estimations put it close to 20–30% of total calories consumed. That means if you eat 100 calories of protein, it would take 20–30 of those calories just to burn the food that you're eating. This is one of the reasons why protein is recommended for weight loss and body composition

goals. It is hard to overeat protein in healthy adults, and it can increase the overall energy expenditure. Carbohydrates are next on the list, and it is believed that 5–10% of carbohydrates is required to burn them up, so from 100 calories of carbohydrates, your

Chapter 2: Understanding Energy Balance (cont.)

body would use 5–10 of them just to digest them. It is believed that complex carbohydrates have a higher thermogenic effect than simple carbohydrates. Your body is very good at absorbing all the nutrients from fats. Fats only have an estimated 0–3% thermogenic effect of food. Strategies to increase your metabolism would be to eat a diet high in protein and complex carbohydrates to take full advantage of the thermogenic effect of food.

Exercise Activity Thermogenesis (EAT) refers to the total amount of energy expended during exercise. Exercise and NEAT are different because NEAT is just all the normal stuff you do every day while exercise is purposeful movement designed to increase some component of your physical fitness.

Resistance training, going for a run, football conditioning, volleyball conditioning, and swimming practice all count as exercise because they are purposeful and structured. Going for a hike or playing a game of basketball with your friends would count as NEAT because they are fun parts of living an active lifestyle. They aren't really structured in any meaningful way. The later chapters will focus much more on exercise activity thermogenesis, but you should know that exercise really only makes up about 10–15% of your total calories burned per day. This is what people mean when they say "you can't outwork a bad diet." If you eat highly processed foods with a ton of calories all the time, you can't expect to work it all off with exercise. While exercise has many benefits, eating poorly and then trying to work it off later will wear you down over time. It is much easier just to make sensible eating decisions and develop healthy relationships with food than trying to work off excess food all the time.

Key Notes
- **Energy Balance** refers to the total amount of energy (calories) being consumed and the total amount of energy being used up by the body.
- **Metabolism** is defined as the chemical processes that occur within a living organism in order to maintain life. There are four major components that make up your **metabolism**, your **basal metabolic rate**, **non-exercise activity thermogenesis**, **thermogenic effect of food**, and **exercise activity thermogenesis**.
  - **Basal Metabolic Rate (BMR)** is the number of calories a person needs per day to continue breathing, circulating blood, maintaining body temperature, and essentially staying alive.
  - **Non-Exercise Activity Thermogenesis (NEAT)** refers to the total amount of calories you burn per day doing basic movements like walking, standing, fidgeting, or even typing.
  - **Thermogenic Effect of Food** refers to the calories it takes to digest, absorb, and metabolize the nutrients in food.
  - **Exercise Activity Thermogenesis (EAT)** refers to the total amount of energy expended during exercise.
- **Total Daily Energy Expenditure (TDEE)** is the sum of all four of these components that make up your metabolism TDEE is the total amount of calories burned doing all of these things. This can be figured using online calculators or by hand to find your rough estimate of calories burned per day.

Chapter 3: Calculating Total Daily Energy Expenditure

Total Daily Energy Expenditure

Total Daily Energy Expenditure (TDEE) is how many calories you burn per day throughout all your daily activities, including all of the previously-mentioned components of metabolism. How many calories it takes just to stay alive (BMR); to walk, brush your teeth, and grocery store shop (NEAT); to digest the food we eat (TEF); and fuel our weightlifting session, soccer practice, or dance recital (EAT). There are many online calculators that will estimate your TDEE based off your height, weight, activity level, and sex. The most popular method is the **Harris-Benedict equation**. This equation uses the metric system so students will have to convert their weight and height into kilograms and centimeters.

1. Calculate your basal metabolic rate (BMR) using the appropriate equation:
   a. Biological males: BMR = 88.362 + (13.397 x weight in kg) + (4.799 x height in cm) - (5.677 x age in years)
   b. Biological females: BMR = 447.593 + (9.247 x weight in kg) + (3.098 x height in cm) - (4.330 x age in years)
2. Determine your activity level using the following scale:
   a. Sedentary (little or no exercise): BMR x 1.2
   b. Lightly Active (light exercise or sports 1–3 days per week): BMR x 1.375
   c. Moderately Active (moderate exercise or sports 3–5 days per week): BMR x 1.55
   d. Very Active (hard exercise or sports 6–7 days per week): ZBMR x 1.725
   e. Super Active (very hard exercise or sports, physical job, or training twice per day): BMR x 1.9
3. Multiply your BMR by the appropriate activity factor to calculate your TDEE.

   So, let's say you are a 27-year-old biological male weighing 90 kg and 180 cm tall.
   a. 27-year-old male, 90 kg, 180 cm
   b. BMR = 88.362 + (13.397 x 90) + (4.799 x 180) - (5.677 x 27)
   c. BMR = 2,004 calories
   Now let's say you are sedentary.
   a. BMR x 1.2
   b. 2,004 x 1.2 = 2,404.8
   Now let's say you are very active.
   a. BMR x 1.725
   b. 2,004 x 1.725 = 3,456.9

   As you can see, the difference between being sedentary and being very active is huge. This is why it's so important to exercise and find active hobbies. It will allow you to burn significantly more calories throughout your days, which will decrease the likelihood of gaining fat as you age, which will also decrease the likelihood of disease as you age.

Chapter 3: Calculating Total Daily Energy Expenditure (cont.)

Try your own calculations based on your weight, height, age, and sex. Keep in mind, if you're still growing, you will likely need more calories than this equation because your body is still trying to grow. In this case, trust your hunger hormones ghrelin and leptin to guide you on when you're hungry and full and try to make sensible eating decisions focusing on highly nutritious whole foods.

Key Points
- **Total Daily Energy Expenditure (TDEE)** is how many calories you burn per day throughout all your daily activities including the sum of your Basal Metabolic Rate, Thermogenic Effect of Food, Non-Exercise Activity Thermogenesis, and Exercise Activity Thermogenesis.
- **Be able to find your own TDEE using the equation above.**
  - ◆ Must be able to convert weight in pounds and height in inches to kilograms and centimeters

Activity: Calculate Your Own TDEE

Instructions for Students: Use the above formula to calculate your own Total Daily Energy Expenditure. Understand that if you're still growing, your daily energy expenditure might be more to accommodate this growth. If you're highly active and participating in sports, your total daily energy expenditure might be more as well.

Knowing how many calories you burn per day is important as a reference point to maintaining healthy body weight, losing body fat, or even gaining muscle. This is very similar to finding your salary at work. You can't possibly learn to budget if you don't know how much money you're making at work. If you work harder, you earn a raise, which increases your salary and the amount of money you can spend. If you exercise and are physically active, you increase your "salary" (how many calories you burn in a day) and can "spend" more (eat more food) without any negative consequences. Also by building muscle, your weight will go up, further increasing your "salary" but in a healthy way because muscle mass has many positive impacts on your health.

Chapter 4: The Importance of Maintaining Healthy Energy Balance

If you are in a **negative calorie balance**, or **calorie deficit**, every day, you will starve to death eventually. If you are in a **positive calorie balance** every day, you will likely gain a lot of unwanted **adipose tissue**, or fat, which can lead to obesity and subsequently cancer, heart disease, and diabetes. Luckily, your body is designed to send signals and let you know when you're hungry and when you've eaten enough food. Your body will release a chemical called **ghrelin** when it senses you need more fuel—this makes you hungry. An easy way to think about this is you turn into a gremlin when you're hungry. People generally get irritable when they're hungry. Another hormone called **leptin** tells you when you've eaten enough food. Your body will release more of this when it has enough calories. By eating slowly, you give your body plenty of time to produce these chemicals and tell you when you should stop eating. If you eat too quickly, your body doesn't have enough time to send the hormones to your brain, which can lead to overeating, getting too full, and having digestive issues from eating so much. This is why it's important to chew your food all the way and eat slowly!

Adipose Tissue

Adipose tissue, or **body fat**, is a connective tissue found in the body and is primarily responsible for storing energy. Body fat is composed of **adipocytes**, which are specialized cells that store fat molecules known as **triglycerides**. Triglycerides can be broken down into energy when food is unavailable or scarce. This has evolutionarily kept us alive through harsh winters and periods of time where food is hard to come by. There are two main types of adipose tissue called **White Adipose Tissue (WAT)** and **Brown Adipose Tissue (BAT)**.

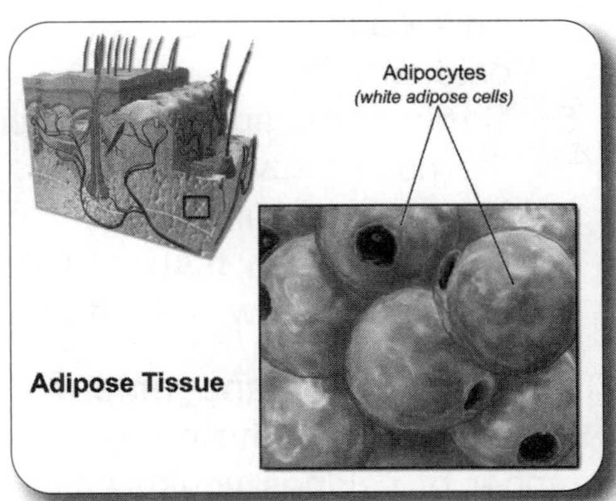

1. **White Adipose Tissue:** White body fat is the most common type of fat in the body. It primarily serves as a source of energy that helps fuel the body when food can't be found or food is scarce. White body fat is primarily found underneath the skin (subcutaneous fat) and around organs (visceral fat).

2. **Brown Adipose Tissue:** Brown body fat is primarily involved in thermogenesis, which generates heat in the body. Brown body fat contains mitochondria, which are your body's powerhouse of the cell and provides energy. Brown tissue is mostly found in newborns and in small amounts around the neck and upper back in adults.

While having healthy amounts of body fat is crucial for energy storage, insulation, protecting organs, and hormone regulation, having too much body fat is known as **obesity** and has detrimental effects on health. It is associated with diabetes, cardiovascular disease, and many cancers.

Obesity

Obesity is a medical condition characterized by an excessive accumulation of body fat that poses a risk to an individual's health. Weight classifications such as underweight, normal weight, overweight, and obese are determined by a person's **body mass index (BMI)**, which is calculated by dividing their weight in kilograms by the square of their height in meters. Having a BMI of 30 or higher is generally considered obese.

Chapter 4: The Importance of Maintaining Healthy Energy Balance (cont.)

Obesity is influenced by a combination of genetic, environmental, and lifestyle factors. Excessive calorie intake paired with sedentary behavior and a lack of physical activity all increase the likelihood of obesity. Some factors you can't control, like genetic factors and socioeconomic status, but it is important to control the things you can control, such as monitoring your caloric intake, living an active lifestyle, and exercising.

Obesity has been associated with having significant negative effects on both physical and mental health. The risk of the following diseases increases significantly:

1. **Cardiovascular Disease:** Including heart disease, high blood pressure, and strokes
2. **Type 2 Diabetes:** Obesity is a major risk factor for developing insulin resistance and type 2 diabetes.
3. **Respiratory Problems:** Excess weight can lead to breathing difficulties such as sleep apnea and impaired sleep, which leads to many other health-related problems.
4. **Joint Problems:** Having excess weight puts additional strain on the joints with all movements. This leads to joints breaking down sooner in life than intended and also increases the risk of osteoarthritis.
5. **Cancer:** Because excess body fat increases systemic inflammation throughout the body, the risk of several cancers, including breast cancer, colon cancer, and pancreatic cancer, increases significantly.
6. **Mental Health Issues:** Obesity can be psychologically damaging as well, increasing the likelihood of low self-esteem, depression, and anxiety.

Tips for Weight Management

By eating **whole foods**, you can increase the amount of nutrients while minimizing the number of calories you're eating. Vegetables have a lot of mass but are very low in calories, meaning you can fill up your stomach with vegetables and you'll get full much faster. Protein and complex carbohydrates containing a lot of fiber also fill you up very fast. Eating whole proteins such as chicken, lean beef, turkey, salmon, and tofu and complex carbohydrates such as whole grains, legumes, and potato starches will increase the amount of food volume and nutrients you eat while keeping your calories down. Eating a highly processed diet such as chips, crackers, cookies, and garlic bread generally has much lower protein, lower fiber, lower vitamins and minerals, and can lead to overeating over time. It is okay to eat these foods in moderation, but these foods are much easier to overeat because they aren't very filling. It will be harder to keep a stable energy balance eating processed food than it will be with whole foods. Apply the 80/20 principle to foods—80 percent of your food should be whole foods while 20 percent of it can be processed foods. It's okay to enjoy a slice of birthday cake at a party, but you probably shouldn't eat birthday cake for every meal all day long.

If you want to increase your metabolism so you can eat more food without gaining weight, there are several ways to do this. By increasing your muscle mass, via strength training and a high protein diet, you will burn more calories throughout the day by increasing your BMR total calories. Also, if you happen to overeat but you're also lifting weights, a lot of those calories will go into building muscle tissue instead of gaining fat, making lifting weights a great strategy for long term health and wellness. By increasing your protein and complex carbohydrate intake, you increase

Chapter 4: The Importance of Maintaining Healthy Energy Balance (cont.)

the thermogenic effect of food, meaning you burn more calories from the food you eat. Look for ways to increase your total steps per day. USDA recommends getting 10,000 steps per day through walk breaks, structured walks, and daily activity. Wearing a step counter and shooting for 10,000–15,000 steps per day is a good way to increase your NEAT calories and burn more calories throughout the day. Going for a run, biking, or doing some other form of structured cardiovascular exercise is also a great way to increase the number of calories you burn via exercise activity thermogenesis.

As you can see, living an active lifestyle is the easiest way to increase the number of calories burned per day. Eating whole nutritious foods is the easiest way to increase the number of vitamins and minerals in your diet without consuming too many extra calories. If you are going to eat in a positive energy balance, it is a good strategy to learn how to lift weights so that a higher percent of the extra calories turns into muscle instead of being stored as fat tissue.

Key Points

- **Negative energy balance**, also known as a **calorie deficit**, is defined as eating fewer calories than you are burning, which results in weight loss.
- **Positive energy balance**, also known as a **calorie surplus**, is defined as eating more calories than you are burning, which results in weight gain.
- **Adipose tissue**, or **fat**, is our body's main source of energy storage. Fat is used to store energy, insulate and regulate body temperature, protect and cushion vital organs, and it regulates hormones such as ghrelin and leptin. Having a healthy amount of body fat is vital to sustain life.
- **Obesity** is a medical condition characterized by an excessive accumulation of body fat that poses a risk to an individual's health. Obesity is influenced by genetic, environmental, and lifestyle factors but is primarily brought on by excessive calorie intake, sedentary behavior, and a lack of physical activity. Obesity increases risk of cardiovascular disease, type 2 diabetes, respiratory problems, joint problems, cancer, and mental health issues.
- **BMI**, or **Body Mass Index**, is calculated by dividing a person's weight in kilograms by the square of their height in meters and is used by doctors and medical health providers to diagnose and treat obesity.
- **Whole foods** refers to eating natural, minimally processed foods that are high in nutrients and low in additives, preservatives, and artificial ingredients.
- **Muscle mass** increases your metabolism and allows you to burn more calories throughout the day. Building muscle mass is a good strategy to prevent fat gain and keep a fast metabolism.
- **10,000 steps per day** is noted by the USDA to offer the most health benefits and maintain body weight. Up to **15,000** steps per day is a great way to lose body weight as well.

Chapter 4: The Importance of Maintaining Healthy Energy Balance (cont.)

Activity: Weight Loss, Weight Maintenance, or Weight Gain Calculations

Instructions for Students: For this activity, it is important to understand a few key concepts. There are 3,500 calories in one pound of body fat and one pound of muscle. This means in order to lose one pound, you must burn 3,500 extra calories in a calorie deficit. To gain one pound, you must eat an additional 3,500 calories. It is almost impossible to burn 3,500 extra calories in one day, and it is almost impossible to eat an extra 3,500 calories per day. So, when you weigh yourself and you weigh a pound or two different every day, don't stress about this because it is mostly fluctuations in your water intake, bowel movements, and other outside factors. Weight loss and weight gain takes weeks and months to accumulate, so don't worry about day-to-day fluctuations as long as over the course of the month your weight is going in the direction you want it.

Suppose you want to lose or gain some weight.* For the purpose of this activity, we will use 1 week as your reference point to either gaining 1 pound, losing 1 pound, or staying the same body weight. It is generally recommended to only try to lose or gain 1 pound per week, as losing weight too quickly can have serious negative health outcomes, and gaining weight too quickly will result in excess fat gain instead of muscle gain.

*These calculations are only for the purposes of this educational activity. You should only start a weight loss or gain program after consulting with a doctor and your parents.

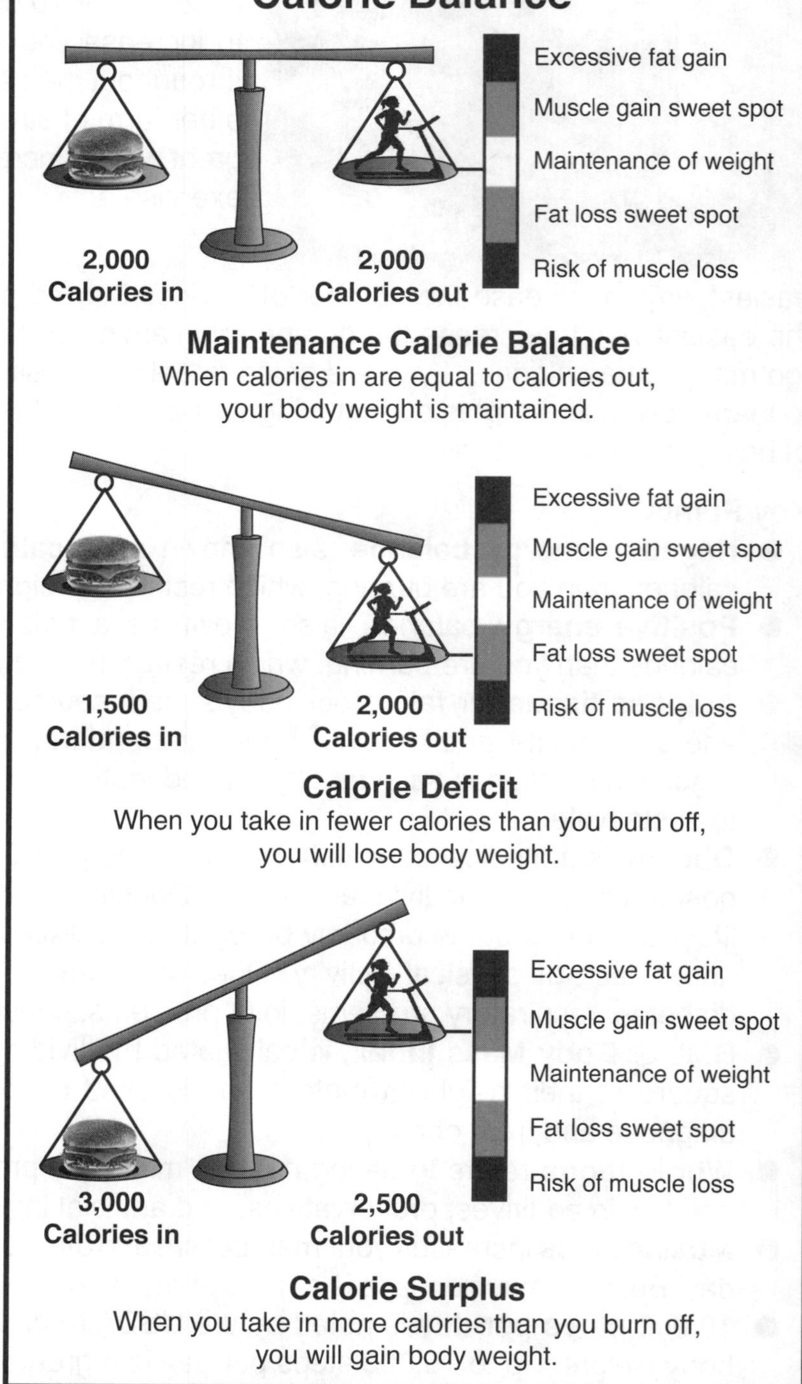

Maintenance Calorie Balance
When calories in are equal to calories out, your body weight is maintained.

Calorie Deficit
When you take in fewer calories than you burn off, you will lose body weight.

Calorie Surplus
When you take in more calories than you burn off, you will gain body weight.

Chapter 4: The Importance of Maintaining Healthy Energy Balance (cont.)

Activity: Weight Loss, Weight Maintenance, or Weight Gain Calculations (cont.)

1. First, decide how much weight you would like to gain, lose, or maintain over the next 6 months.
   a. Keep in mind the rules for the assignment. You can only gain or lose 1 pound per week.

2. Next, record your TDEE (Total Daily Energy Expenditure) you found in the previous activity. That is your baseline for how many calories you typically burn per day.

3. Remember, there are 3,500 calories in one pound. There are 4 weeks per month and the activity calls for 6 months, which translates to 24 total weeks.

4. Multiply the pounds you want to gain or lose by the total amount of calories in a pound (3,500). That is how many total extra calories you will have to burn/eat OVER your TDEE to reach your goals.

5. Next, divide the total calories by how many weeks you have to reach your goal (24 weeks). This is how many calories per week you will have to either burn or eat depending on your goals.

6. Divide the total calories needed by 7 because there are 7 days in a week. This is your average calorie deficit/surplus per day.

7. Finally, subtract (if weight loss) or add (if weight gain) this number of calories to your overall TDEE to find how many calories you will have to eat per day to reach your goal, whether that's weight gain or weight loss.

Example 1: I weigh 200 pounds, and I want to lose 24 pounds over the next 6 months.

1. I want to lose 24 pounds, which is 24 x 3,500 = 84,000 less calories over the next 6 months.
2. My TDEE I calculated in the last activity was 2,700.
3. There are 24 total weeks in the next 6 months, and there are 3,500 calories in a pound. I want to lose 24 pounds in 24 weeks, which equals 1 pound per week.
4. Because I want to lose 1 pound per week and there are 3,500 calories in a pound, I will have to eat 3,500 fewer calories per week to lose 1 pound per week.
5. 3,500 calories divided by 7 days = 500 fewer calories per day.
6. My TDEE is 2,700 so I have to subtract 500 calories from this to find how many calories per day I should be eating, which is 2,200 calories.
7. Based on this, I should be eating close to 2,200 calories per day, every day for the next 6 months to lose 24 pounds.
8. It is important to note that you should redo this equation every time weight loss slows. The less you weigh, the lower your TDEE, so these calculations will need to be adjusted every couple of months to ensure you are continually losing weight until you reach your goal.

Chapter 4: The Importance of Maintaining Healthy Energy Balance (cont.)

Activity: Weight Loss, Weight Maintenance, or Weight Gain Calculations (cont.)

Example 2: I weigh 200 pounds, and I want to gain 10 pounds of muscle over the next 6 months.

1. I want to gain 10 pounds, which is 10 x 3,500 = 35,000 extra calories over the next 6 months.
2. My TDEE is 2,700 calories.
3. 35,000/24 (because I have 24 weeks to reach my goal) is 1,458 extra calories per week over the 24-week period.
4. 1,458 calories divided by 7 days is 208 extra calories per day.
5. My TDEE is 2,700, so I have to add 208 calories per day to gain the weight I would like to gain per day.
6. In order to gain 10 pounds over the next 6 months, I would have to eat 2,908 calories per day. In order to make sure this is muscle mass and not fat mass, I will also have to resistance train.

The purpose of this exercise is to help teens understand that your goals take time and don't occur overnight. Whether you're trying to gain weight for sports or lose weight for health purposes, this oftentimes takes months or even years to do. There are no shortcuts. Crash dieting/starving yourself to lose weight or binge eating to gain weight will only help to create eating disorders. It's important for teenagers to learn just how long it takes to actually lose/gain a substantial amount of weight, especially since so many fake weight loss fad diets pop up every year. Weight loss is simply an equation over time, and understanding the equation and your TDEE will help you reach your goals.

Building a Healthy Diet

Chapter 5: Choosing Your Foods Via MyPlate

MyPlate

MyPlate is the visual representation of the five food groups the United States Department of Agriculture (USDA) recommends that people eat for a healthy, balanced diet. It was designed to replace the food pyramid in 2011 as new information and science came to light about the food groups. MyPlate is a flexible tool that you can use to help plan out your meals and guide you to make healthy food choices. Develop a personalized food plan at <myplate.gov>.

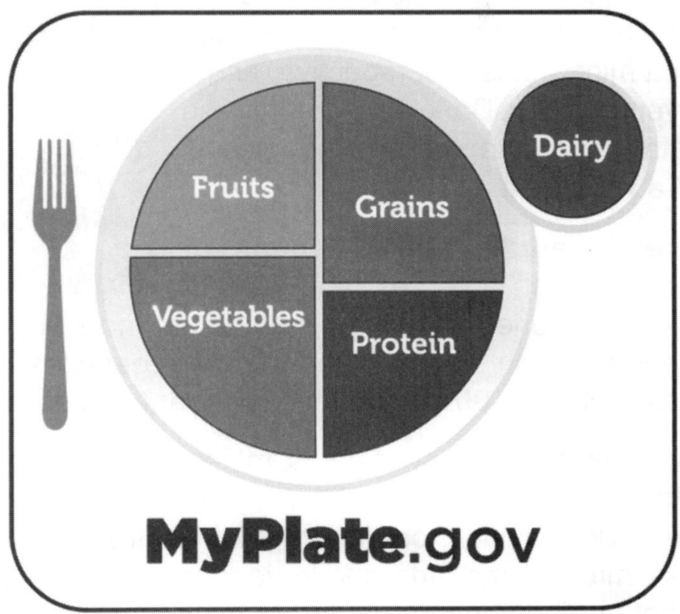

As you can see, this visual demonstration is very easily applied to your own plate at lunch or dinner. This aligns very well with the previous chapters, eating a diet high in protein (protein and dairy), complex carbohydrates (grains and vegetables), simple carbohydrates (fruits), and getting adequate fat (also typically from protein and dairy).

Fruits

Fruits are considered simple carbohydrates. Remember, simple carbohydrates are typically "fast energy" and digested very quickly. This makes them perfect before a strenuous workout, practice, or game. Fruit contains a ton of vitamins as well, which makes it highly nutritious. Most fruits have a lot of fiber too, helping you stay full, which also makes them a great snack. Along with vitamins and minerals, fruit contains plenty of antioxidants. Fruit juice, however, is usually stripped of the fiber and highly concentrates the sugars into a liquid. While it's hard to overeat fruit, it is very easy to drink too much fruit juice and spike your blood sugar. Try to eat as much of your fruit from whole sources as possible.

Chapter 5: Choosing Your Foods Via MyPlate (cont.)

MyPlate recommends adults consume 1.5–2 cups of fruit per day. Canned and frozen fruits are a great way to get your fruit because they are more affordable since fresh fruit can be more expensive. One cup of fruit can equal 1 cup fresh, frozen, or canned fruit; 1 cup 100% fruit juice; or 1/2 cup dried fruit. If you are very active, you might need more than 1.5–2 cups of fruit per day. Adjust servings to fit with your total calories burned per day, like we discussed in the last chapter.

Vegetables

Vegetables are considered complex carbohydrates. They contain a lot of micronutrients, are typically very low in calories, and have a lot of fiber. This means they fill you up, keep you nourished from a micronutrient perspective, and it is almost impossible to overeat them. Dark leafy greens, red and orange vegetables, starchy vegetables, and legumes all fall under the umbrella of a vegetable.

MyPlate recommends adults eat 2–3 cups of vegetables per day, depending on age, sex, and level of activity. If you're burning more calories, you might want to eat more vegetables. If you're burning less, you don't have to eat as much volume. One cup of vegetables could mean 1 cup fresh, frozen, or canned vegetables; 1 cup 100% vegetable juice; or 2 cups leafy salad greens.

Different vegetables provide different vitamins, minerals, antioxidants, and phytochemicals. This is why it's so important to eat a variety of different vegetables. Try to "eat the rainbow" and eat some dark leafy greens like spinach, orange vegetables like carrots, yellow vegetables like corn, white vegetables like mushrooms, and purple vegetables like eggplant. Different colors of vegetables contain different nutrients, so try not to eat the same kind every day as they all have their own benefits.

Grains

Grains are technically the seeds of grass-like plants such as wheat, rice, oats, rye, buckwheat, corn, and barley. Foods made from these grains include bread, pasta, tortillas, breakfast cereals, and grits. Other foods included in the grains group are oatmeal, rice, and popcorn. Grains provide

many nutrients such as complex carbohydrates, dietary fiber, B vitamins, iron, magnesium, and selenium. Fiber may lower the risk of heart disease by lowering blood cholesterol levels. The B vitamins are important for metabolism. Adequate iron helps maintain healthy oxygen levels in the blood.

There are two types of grains used in foods: whole grains and refined grains. **Whole grains** contain the whole grain kernel, which includes the bran, germ, and endosperm. The bran is the outer shell of the kernel that contains fiber, B vitamins, and trace minerals. The germ provides antioxidants, vitamin E, and B vitamins. The endosperm provides energy with carbohydrates and protein. Examples of whole grains are whole-wheat flour, bulgur (cracked wheat), oatmeal, and brown rice. **Refined grains**

Chapter 5: Choosing Your Foods Via MyPlate (cont.)

have been processed to remove the bran and the germ. This gives the grain products a smoother texture, but it removes the dietary fiber, iron, and many of the B vitamins. Refined grain products include white flour, white bread, corn grits, and white rice. Refined grains are usually **enriched** by adding B vitamins (thiamin, riboflavin, niacin, folic acid) and iron back into the food. Many food products are made from a mixture of whole and refined grains. Check the label for whole grains listed first in the ingredients list.

MyPlate recommends adults eat approximately 7–10 ounces of grains, depending on age, sex, and level of activity, with half of those grains being whole grains. An ounce of grains is equivalent to 1 slice of bread; 1/2 cup cooked pasta, rice, or cereal; 1 (6-in.) tortilla; 1 (5-in.) pancake; or 1 cup of cereal flakes.

Protein

Protein is a very important part of MyPlate, especially for growing children and athletes. Remember, protein makes up your muscle, tendon, ligaments, organs, hair, skin, and nails. While you're growing, you're creating more of these tissues. That makes it very important to get an adequate amount of protein. While you're exercising, your body breaks down some of your muscle mass. It is important to eat enough protein to replace this breakdown. This is one of the reasons wrestlers and football players lose so much weight during the season—they aren't eating enough protein in their diets. If you're getting your protein from animal sources, typically that protein will have sufficient fat content in it as well. For instance, beef, eggs, salmon, and lamb all have protein and fat within them so you can cover both of your dietary needs, fat and protein, in the protein section of your plate. Also, generally speaking, people cook in various types of oils. When you cook meat, generally you'll use butter, ghee, or olive oil. These oils are healthy fats, which coat the meat for cooking and give it its flavor. That is one of the ways you obtain your fats from the MyPlate recommendation.

MyPlate recommends 5–7 ounces of protein per day. Again, this is highly dependent on your age, sex, weight, activity level, and if you're still growing. If you are highly active and have a lot of muscle mass, you will need much more protein. If you're still growing, you will need more protein to make those tissues. If you are sedentary and don't work out, you don't need as much protein per day. One ounce of protein could be equal to 1 ounce of lean meat, poultry, or seafood; 1 egg; 1 tablespoon peanut butter; 1/2 ounce nuts or seeds; or 1/4 cup cooked beans, peas, or lentils.

Fish, eggs, meat, poultry, legumes, tofu, and pea protein all contain different amounts of amino acids. Remember, amino acids are the building blocks of protein. Similar to vegetables containing different types of nutrients in them, you have to eat a wide variety of protein sources to make sure you're getting all the vitamins, minerals, and amino acids that your body needs. If you only eat chicken for example, you will miss out on the iron found in red meat. If you only eat red meat, you will miss out on the omega-3 fatty acids found in salmon and other types of fish. Like everything, balance and variety are key.

Chapter 5: Choosing Your Foods Via MyPlate (cont.)

Dairy

Dairy is the final important piece of the MyPlate puzzle. Dairy contains vitamins, antioxidants, minerals, fat, protein, and some carbohydrates. Dairy is loaded with calcium that our body then uses to make our teeth and bones, which is especially important as you're growing. **MyPlate recommends 3 cups of dairy per day.** A cup of dairy could be equal to 1 cup of milk, 1 cup of soy milk (fortified soy beverage), 1 cup of yogurt, or 1.5 ounces of natural cheese.

Dairy isn't just milk. Dairy is also yogurt, fortified soy milk, cheese, and pudding. Dairy is very high in Vitamin D as well, which is important for bone health, muscle function, and overall hormonal health. Along with dairy comes fat and protein, so that is another way you can eat your fat calories using the MyPlate visual representation. Thanks to new filtration methods, many milks and cheeses can now be purchased lactose free for those of you with lactose intolerance.

Vegetarian and Vegan Diets

Many people are choosing to follow vegetarian or vegan diets. This may be for health reasons to avoid high fat or high cholesterol foods, such as animal proteins and dairy products. They may also have ethical concerns about consuming and using animal products. Whatever the case, those who follow a vegetarian or vegan diet must make sure to get the proper amount of nurtients from other food sources. A wide variety of plant-based foods are available with options that taste like meat, eggs, milk, or cheese. Vitamin and mineral supplements may also be necessary to replace those nutrients that plant-based foods do not include. Anyone on a vegetarian or vegan diet should consult their physician or a dietician to make a healthy plan.

Vegan sausages, coffee latte, and muffin

You may have heard the terms vegetarian and vegan, but do you know the difference? Here are some definitions for the different types of vegetarians.

Vegan: excludes all meat and animal products. Vegans also will not use animal products like leather, silk, or fur.

Vegetarian: excludes all meat but will eat dairy and eggs.

Lacto-Vegetarian: eats dairy but no eggs.

Ovo-Vegetarian: eats eggs but no dairy.

Lacto-Ovo-Vegetarian: eats eggs and dairy.

Pescatarian: avoids meats and poultry but does eat fish.

Flexitarian: primarily vegetarian but will occasionally eat meat and fish.

Chapter 5: Choosing Your Foods Via MyPlate (cont.)

Key Points

- **MyPlate** is the visual representation of the five food groups the United States Department of Agriculture (USDA) recommends that people eat for a healthy, balanced diet.
  - ◆ MyPlate is further divided into fruit, vegetables, protein, grains, and dairy.
- **Fruits** are considered simple carbohydrates. Remember, simple carbohydrates are typically "fast energy" and digested very quickly.
  - ◆ MyPlate recommends adults consume **1.5–2 cups of fruit per day.**
- **Vegetables** are considered complex carbohydrates. They contain a lot of micronutrients, are typically very low in calories, and have a lot of fiber.
  - ◆ MyPlate recommends adults eat **2–3 cups of vegetables per day.**
- **Grains** provide many nutrients such as complex carbohydrates, dietary fiber, B vitamins, iron, magnesium, and selenium.
  - ◆ MyPlate recommends adults eat **7–10 ounces of grains per day.** Half of the grains should be whole grains.
- **Protein** is a very important part of MyPlate, especially for growing children and athletes. Remember, protein makes up your muscle, tendons, ligaments, organs, hair, skin, and nails. While you're growing, you're creating more of these tissues.
  - ◆ MyPlate recommends **5–7 ounces of protein per day.**
- **Dairy** contains vitamins, antioxidants, minerals, fat, protein, and some carbohydrates.
  - ◆ MyPlate recommends **3 cups of dairy per day.**
- **Vegetarian and Vegan Diets**
  - ◆ Types of Vegetarians

Activity 4: Build Your Own Plate

Instructions for Students: For this activity, bring in a circular paper or foam plate from home or your teacher may provide you with one. Bring the plate with you to the cafeteria, where trays or plates are typically rectangular. Distribute the school lunch on the round plate into the different categories

according to the MyPlate diagram. If you bring your own lunch to school, take your lunch and break it down and compare it to the MyPlate recommendations. Are the serving sizes appropriate according to each plate? Do they have enough vegetables? Enough protein? Are they missing dairy? Compare what the lunch is missing or might have too much of and then brainstorm other alternatives or ways to make your lunches better according to the MyPlate recommendations.

Chapter 6: Meal Planning and Preparation

Meal Planning Foundation

Meal planning can be defined as the process of organizing and preparing meals for a certain period of time. Meal planning is an essential habit to learn early on in life for a variety of reasons, including eating healthy and planning financially. Most adults grocery shop once per week so they generally have to plan out everything they're going to eat that week. This is a much better strategy than going to the store blind and getting whatever you feel like getting at the time. Food tends to expire before you get to it or you don't always make the healthiest decisions when you impulse buy what you are craving. By planning out your meals for the week, you can also price match and look for good deals at your local grocery stores. This can save you a lot of money throughout the year planning out your meals based on what's for sale each week. Along with this, you can make sure that the food you make and prepare aligns with your goals, whether that's weight loss, weight maintenance, or weight gain. Before shopping, it is important to discuss your meal plan with your parents and obtain permission to plan, shop, and cook. We encourage you to make this a family activity so the entire process is more enjoyable.

Meal planning begins by picking out the meals you want to make that week. If you're eating predominantly whole foods, you'll need all the ingredients listed for each recipe, which includes plenty of spices for every dish. Eating whole foods doesn't have to be boring! Making your list and sticking to the list will ensure you have everything you need for every recipe you intend on making, will have enough meals to last the entire week, and allow you to go to different stores to find the best deals if need be to make it as cost efficient as possible.

Breaking Down Your Meals

Assuming you like to eat three square meals a day and have two snacks, your meal plan for the school or work week would consist of 15 total meals and 10 snacks. Your recipes and meal planning should reflect your needs. Let's assume you calculated your TDEE and you have to eat 2,500 calories per day to stay the same weight. You want to maintain a balanced ratio of macronutrients consisting of 40% carbs, 30% protein, and 20% fat calories. You would multiply your total allowed calories per day (or your "budget of calories") by the percentages to find out how many calories of each macronutrient you need, then divide that number by the grams associated with that nutrient. Remember, there are 4 calories in 1 gram of protein and carbohydrate and there are 9 calories in 1 gram of fat.

Carbohydrates: 2,500 x 0.4 = 1,000 calories

1,000 calories / 4 = 250 grams of carbs per day

Protein: 2,500 x 0.3 = 750 calories

750 calories / 4 = 187.5 grams of protein per day

Fat: 2,500 x 0.2 = 500 calories

500 / 9 = 55.55 grams of fat per day

Breaking down your macronutrient goals per day is very important to ensure you're eating enough protein, carbohydrates, and fat. This is your calorie budget. Remember, if you eat too little for too long, your body will slowly deteriorate. If you eat too much for too long, you will probably gain unwanted body fat and increase your risk of disease. If you want to grow rich, you start with

Chapter 6: Meal Planning and Preparation (cont.)

a budget, otherwise you risk spending too much and losing all your money. Eating is exactly the same. You want to have a rough estimate of your calorie needs per day and your macronutrient needs to maintain a healthy body composition. Guessing every week does not work. An estimated 70 million adults are obese in the United States, and an estimated 99 million are overweight. Nearly 70% of the country is now overweight or obese. Most individuals must keep track of their budgeted calories in order to stay at a healthy body weight and composition.

Now that you know how many grams of carbohydrates, protein, and fat you need per day, you can break down that total by the amount of meals and snacks you're going to eat every day. Remember back in the earlier example, we wanted 3 meals a day and 2 snacks per day. That equates to roughly 5 meals per day. You can break down each meal by dividing the grams of everything by how many meals you're planning to eat.

250 grams of carbohydrates / 5 meals = 50 grams of carbohydrate per meal

187.5 grams of protein / 5 meals = 46.8 grams of protein per meal

55.55 grams of fat / 5 meals = 11.11 grams of fat per meal

When looking up recipes, you simply look for recipes that reflect your individual needs based on your goals. Not every meal has to be perfect. For instance, some days you might eat a bigger lunch and because of this you don't need to eat a snack. Some days you may eat more fat than you were supposed to, but you end up eating less carbs. This is totally okay as long as you're still roughly eating 2,500 calories. That is the most important factor for staying the same weight. Not every recipe will be perfect either. You will probably have to experiment with different recipes, swapping out different ingredients to make them fit within your macronutrients. Generally, however, if you're eating a wide variety of whole foods, you will have no problem reaching your goals. Here is one example of a day's worth of meals according to this macronutrient breakdown:

Meal 1 (Breakfast):
- 2 large eggs (140 calories, 12 g protein, 1 g carbs, 10 g fat)
- 2 slices of whole grain toast (220 calories, 10 g protein, 36 g carbs, 4 g fat)
- 1 medium banana (105 calories, 1 g protein, 27 g carbs, 0 g fat)
- 1 tablespoon of peanut butter (90 calories, 4 g protein, 3 g carbs, 8 g fat)
- Total: 555 calories, 27 g protein, 67 g carbs, 22 g fat

Meal 2 (Snack):
- 1 apple (95 calories, 0 g protein, 25 g carbs, 0 g fat)
- 1/4 cup of almonds (207 calories, 8 g protein, 8 g carbs, 18 g fat)
- Total: 302 calories, 8 g protein, 33 g carbs, 18 g fat

Meal 3 (Lunch):
- 4 oz grilled chicken breast (140 calories, 28 g protein, 0 g carbs, 2 g fat)
- 1 cup cooked brown rice (218 calories, 5g protein, 45 g carbs, 2 g fat)
- 1 cup steamed broccoli (55 calories, 4 g protein, 11 g carbs, 1 g fat)
- 1 tablespoon olive oil (120 calories, 0 g protein, 0 g carbs, 14 g fat)
- Total: 533 calories, 37 g protein, 56 g carbs, 19 g fat

Chapter 6: Meal Planning and Preparation (cont.)

Meal 4 (Snack):
- 1/2 cup low-fat cottage cheese (80 calories, 14 g protein, 3 g carbs, 1 g fat)
- 1 cup mixed berries (70 calories, 1 g protein, 17 g carbs, 0 g fat)
- Total: 150 calories, 15 g protein, 20 g carbs, 1 g fat

Meal 5 (Dinner):
- 4 oz grilled salmon (233 calories, 25 g protein, 0 g carbs, 14 g fat)
- 1 medium sweet potato (103 calories, 2 g protein, 24 g carbs, 0 g fat)
- 1 cup steamed asparagus (40 calories, 4 g protein, 8 g carbs, 0 g fat)
- 1 tablespoon of butter (102 calories, 0 g protein, 0 g carbs, 12 g fat)
- Total: 478 calories, 31 g protein, 32 g carbs, 26 g fat

Overall totals:
- Calories: 2,518 calories
- Carbohydrates: 253 g
- Protein: 187 g
- Fat: 86 g

This probably seems like a lot of work, but thanks to the advent of meal tracking apps, you can scan most nutrition labels into food tracking apps and they'll pull up the entire nutrition label. With most apps today, you can put in your height, weight, sex, and activity level, and it will estimate how many calories you need per day. You will also be able to adjust protein, carbohydrates, and fat within most apps as well. Most recipes you find online will also have the total calories, protein, carbs, and fat listed. Because of the obesity crisis, tracking nutrition has never been easier—most apps are even free!

This sample provided is just one day full of meals. Generally, people get caught up in life and typically tend to eat the same things over and over again, especially with a busy lifestyle. This makes shopping and calorie counting easier. Furthermore, you can see each meal has a protein, vegetable or fruit, and milk. If you don't want to go through the trouble of tracking or say you're out to eat somewhere where you don't know how much of what you're eating—don't worry, just follow the general guidelines of the visual representation of MyPlate. You can see most of the meals have a protein source, vegetable or fruit, whole grain, and then dairy. As long as each meal consists of the majority of these five groups and you eat a variety of different types of foods throughout the day, you won't become majorly malnourished.

Meal Prepping Tips

Now that you have planned out your meals for the week, put together your shopping list, and ensured that your meals fit within your dietary needs, it's time to cook your food. This is known as **meal prepping**, which generally consists of cooking multiple meals at once. This saves a lot of time, especially if you're cooking for more than just yourself. By cooking in bulk, you can portion the meals out more easily, and you will always have meals on hand.

1. **Plan ahead:** this was covered in the beginning of the section. Find recipes that are easy to prepare and can be made in bulk. Look at your local grocery stores for bargains on vegetables and protein.

Chapter 6: Meal Planning and Preparation (cont.)

2. **Invest in quality containers:** find containers that are freezer, microwave, and dishwasher safe. This will ensure your food stays air tight and you can reheat the food through the week. Look for BPA-free containers.

3. **Use your refrigerator and freezer:** some meals can be frozen and then warmed up later in the oven or slow cooker down the road. Casseroles and lasagna are an easy example of this. Do the work once and then you can just heat up your food when you're too busy to cook during the week. This will also help make sure your food doesn't go bad by the end of the week!

4. **Keep it simple:** If you're new to cooking, don't overcomplicate dishes. Find whole food recipes, get good at the basics, and use plenty of seasoning.

5. **Make sure you have all the right tools**—knives, cutting boards, kitchen utensils—everything you'll need. Set them all out before you begin cooking.

6. **Get all your ingredients out and put them together in the order that the recipe calls for.** Treat cooking like an assembly line—go from one station to the next.

7. **Have on-the-go snacks** like fruit, protein shakes, multi grain bars, hard boiled eggs, etc. all lined up in case you have to eat on the go.

8. **Enjoy finding recipes and making things from scratch!** It's a valuable skill to have, and it will also save you a ton of money rather than eating out for every meal. You also can control how much oil and seasoning you use when you're the chef, so however you like it, you can make it!

Key Notes

- **Meal planning** can be defined as the process of organizing and preparing meals for a certain period of time.
    - ◆ This is a strategic plan based on your meal needs, calorie needs, and macronutrient needs, which will need to be calculated prior to grocery shopping.
- A **grocery list** is your list of food items that meet your dietary goals and needs based on your strategic plan.
    - ◆ When you go to the store without a list, you risk buying things you don't really need via impulse buying and forget things you do need to make your recipes for the week.
    - ◆ You can also shop around and find the best deals on specific foods for your meal plan and save money.
- **Meal prepping** is a useful way to make multiple meals out of your groceries so you save more time throughout the week on cooking, and you only eat the meals that will help you reach your goals.

Chapter 6: Meal Planning and Preparation (cont.)

Activity: Let's Go Shopping

Instructions for the Teacher:

For this activity, have students bring in the local advertising shopper or newspaper that lists the weekly specials at their local stores. If your city doesn't have a local shopper, go to your shopping market's own website and look for deals on healthy foods. Often times, you'll find sales on pork chops, chicken, potatoes, and other whole foods. A common misconception is that eating healthy is expensive. This is not true. Eating out at fast food restaurants or convenience stores is extremely

expensive. You're just paying for things more frequently so your bill is smaller each visit. Convenience stores and restaurants heavily mark up the cost of foods to accommodate convenience and making the food themselves. By buying in bulk and looking for local deals, you can save money because food is significantly less expensive. Rice and potatoes, for example, are ridiculously cheap sources of carbohydrates you can add to most meals. By looking for deals on protein, you can save money according to the deals that week.

Give the students an imaginary budget and help them try to pick food choices and deals that will reflect this budget. Try to encourage teens to follow the 80/20 principle: 80 percent of their food choices should be whole foods (one-ingredient foods such as blueberries, broccoli, bananas, rice, chicken, lean beef, pork chops, eggs, milk) and 20 percent of their food choices "fun" choices like noodles, ice cream, frozen pizza, etc. The majority of the deals will be on whole food choices.

After finding your local deals, help the students create their meal plans or find some recipes they would like to cook after deciding what to buy on sale. If pork loin is on sale, they can look up recipes using pork loin. This encourages the teens to find many different ways to cook the same ingredients, making cooking and meal planning much more fun.

To summarize:
1. Use your local shopper or websites to find the deals in the area where you would like to shop.
2. Give a reasonable budget to the children based on your demographics.
3. Have them create a shopping list following the 80/20 principle for food.
4. Find easy recipes that coincide with the weekly bargains.
5. For this exercise, they don't have to know how to make the food. It's important that they just be able to find food bargains, make reasonable choices, and find recipes that reflect those food choices for the week. From there, if possible their parents can help them actually shop and create the dish—creating a fun family activity at home that will help them bond and build self-efficacy in the kitchen.

Exercise

Chapter 7: Understanding Exercise

Exercise can be defined as physical activity that is planned, structured, and repetitive for the purpose of improving or maintaining some realm of physical fitness, health, and well-being. The American College of Sports Medicine (ACSM) breaks down **physical fitness** into five health-related components:

1. **Body Composition:** Proportion of fat, muscle, and bone in the body and is generally expressed as the percentage of body fat relative to total body weight (body fat percentage), and is an important indicator of overall health and fitness.
2. **Muscular Strength:** Refers to the ability of a muscle or group of muscles to generate maximal force against resistance in a single effort, or one time.
3. **Muscular Endurance:** Refers to the ability of a muscle or a group of muscles to sustain repeated contractions or maintain particular posture over time, essentially how long you can do something.
4. **Flexibility & Mobility:** Refers to the range of motion around a joint or a series of joints and is determined by the length and elasticity of muscles, tendons, and other connective tissues.
5. **Cardiorespiratory Fitness:** Cardiovascular fitness refers to the ability of the heart, lungs, and blood vessels to deliver oxygen and nutrients to the muscles being worked during exercise and physical activity.

Exercise should be designed to increase one of these components of physical fitness. **Physical activity**, or play/recreation, is enjoyable, engaging, and usually done for the purpose of relaxation or entertainment. Physical activity, according to the American College of Sports Medicine (ACSM), is defined as any bodily movement produced by the contraction of skeletal

muscles that results in a substantial increase in calorie requirements. While playing a pickup game of basketball with some friends does improve your cardiorespiratory fitness, it is neither structured nor purposely intended to do so, so that would make that game simply physical activity, or recreation. When you are lifting weights, you are generally trying to improve body composition, muscular strength, muscular endurance, or flexibility, which would count as exercise. There is a lot of overlap between the two. It is important to exercise with the intent to improve these different realms of physical fitness, but it is also important to have fun in life and play games, play golf, play volleyball, play at the park, play in the pool, and do other physically active things. In fact, exercise and improving and maintaining your health is the key to being able to play recreational sports longer. Exercise will help keep you healthier so you can play basketball and volleyball longer in life.

It is important to note that physical activity gets your heart rate up and burns a significant number of calories that will still improve your health in a variety of ways, but for the purpose of this book, we will focus on exercise separate from physical activity.

Chapter 7: Understanding Exercise (cont.)

Benefits of Being Physically Fit

There are many benefits to being physically fit. Cardiovascular exercise strengthens the heart, improves blood flow, and reduces the risk of heart disease and stroke. Resistance training increases muscle strength and endurance, improves body composition, makes your bones stronger, and subsequently lowers the risk of diabetes, osteoporosis, and everyday fractures. Exercise reduces stress, anxiety, and depression as well as improves mood and general outlook on life. People who exercise typically have an easier time falling asleep, which also improves your quality of life. Exercise increases your day-to-day energy and stamina, improves cognitive function, and increases lifespan. Exercise is the single best medication you can take!

Exercise Types

There are three main types of exercises, all of which improve physical fitness in different ways. **Aerobic/cardiovascular exercise**, **anaerobic/resistance training exercise**, and **flexibility/mobility training** are the three major modes of exercise. Each has distinct benefits, some overlap, and the ACSM has guidelines on how much and how often to do each per week.

Aerobic means requiring oxygen, so aerobic exercises are exercises that require large amounts of oxygen and fat/carbohydrates. Because oxygen is transported through your cardiovascular and respiratory system, aerobic exercise is also known as cardiovascular exercise because it improves your body's ability to use oxygen. Oxygen is like coal in a fire, we use it to produce energy to do all kinds of things.

Aerobic Exercise Examples

- Running
- Jogging
- Cycling
- Swimming
- Jumping rope
- Rowing
- Brisk walking
- Stair climbing
- Dance classes

Anaerobic means not requiring oxygen. These are short bursts of very intense exercise. Your body mostly burns creatine and sugar as fuel.

Anaerobic Exercise Examples

- Weightlifting
- Sprinting
- Plyometric exercises (repeated rapid stretching and contracting of muscles, as by jumping and rebounding)
- Agility Drills
- Powerlifting
- CrossFit
- Calisthenics (Bodyweight)

Chapter 7: Understanding Exercise (cont.)

Flexibility training does not burn a significant amount of fuel, but instead aims to improve range of motion and flexibility of the muscles and joints.

Flexibility Training Examples
- Static Stretching
- Dynamic Stretching
- Passive/Active Stretching
- Yoga
- Pilates
- Foam Rolling

Key Points
- **Exercise** can be defined as physical activity that is planned, structured, and repetitive for the purpose of improving or maintaining some realm of physical fitness, health, and well-being.
  - ◆ **Designed to improve one or more of the following components of physical fitness:**
    - ❏ **Body Composition**
    - ❏ **Muscular Strength**
    - ❏ **Muscular Endurance**
    - ❏ **Flexibility & Mobility**
    - ❏ **Cardiorespiratory Fitness**
- **Physical activity** is defined as any bodily movement produced by the contraction of skeletal muscles that results in a substantial increase in calorie requirements.
- **Aerobic exercise**, or cardiovascular exercise, is defined as physical activity that involves continuous and rhythmic movements designed to increase oxygen consumption and improve cardiorespiratory fitness.
- **Anaerobic exercise** is defined as physical activity that involves intense, short bursts of exercise where the demands of exercise exceed the oxygen supply so the body must burn off carbohydrates instead of oxygen for fuel.
- **Flexibility training** is designed to improve range of motion and flexibility of the muscles and joints.

Chapter 7: Understanding Exercise (cont.)

Activity: Testing Your Fitness

Physical fitness can be divided into 5 components: body composition, muscular strength, muscular endurance, cardiovascular health, and flexibility.

Testing Body Composition

Instructions for Students:

The most affordable way to measure body composition, or body fat percentage, is by using and measuring with **skin fold calipers**. These can be purchased from online retailers and are extremely affordable. Once obtained, students can all use the same calipers and share when their turn is over. Calipers provide a rough estimate of body fat. Use a **three-point skinfold test** to measure body fat percentage. This involves measuring the thickness of three skinfold sites on the body. Underwater weighing, bod pod measurements, and DEXA scans are all more reliable. More and more at home scales are being built with body fat percent testers, which can be inaccurate according to water fluctuations. However, skin calipers are one of the most tested and universal methods for testing body composition, but they do require some practice.

For Males:
1. **Chest (pectoral) Skinfold:** Measure the diagonal fold on the front of the chest, midway between the nipple and the upper edge of the armpit (axilla).
2. **Abdominal Skinfold:** Measure the vertical fold taken 2 cm to the right side of the belly button (umbilicus).
3. **Thigh Skinfold:** Measure the vertical fold on the front of the thigh, midway between the hip and knee joints.

For Females:
1. **Triceps Skinfold:** Measure the vertical fold on the back of the upper arm, halfway between the shoulder and elbow.
2. **Suprailiac Skinfold:** Measure the diagonal fold just above the crest of the hip bone, at a 45-degree angle.
3. **Thigh Skinfold:** Measure the vertical fold on the front of the thigh, midway between the hip and knee joints.

Procedure:
1. The skinfold measurements should be taken on the right side of the body.
2. Use the thumb and forefinger to pinch the skin and subcutaneous fat at each site, ensuring that only the skin and fat tissue are grasped.
3. Apply the calipers approximately 1 cm above the pinch site, perpendicular to the skinfold, and release the caliper handles to measure the skinfold thickness.
4. Take each measurement in duplicate and retest if there is a significant difference between the two measurements.
5. Record the measurements in millimeters (mm).
6. Use an appropriate equation or body fat percentage calculator that considers age and gender to estimate the body fat percentage based on the sum of the skinfold measurements.

Chapter 7: Understanding Exercise (cont.)

Activity: Testing Your Fitness (cont.)

Testing Muscular Strength

Instructions for Students:

The **One-Rep Maximum (1RM) Test** is the most common way to test muscular strength. This means warming up with bench press, squat, or deadlift up to your **top set**, which is the most amount of weight you can do with good form one time. These are used in sports testing. The biggest problem with this test is it requires equipment and skill to know how to bench press, squat, or deadlift. For this reason, if you have access to a gym, it may be easier to test your one-rep max with a leg press or leg extension to evaluate lower body strength and a chest press machine to establish upper body strength. If you have access to equipment, be careful to warm up prior to throwing weight on and testing your one rep. Perform 10 reps (repetitions) of an easy weight you know you can do, then slowly add weight in increments testing one rep at a time. Ideally wait 2–5 minutes in between testing bouts. It works well to test muscle strength by having one teen go after another, rotating and circling back when the rotation is complete. If you don't feel comfortable testing muscular strength or don't have the equipment, please skip this activity.

Testing Muscular Endurance

Instructions for Students:

The most common way to test muscular endurance is the **60-second pushup test**. It measures the number of push-ups a person can perform consecutively before reaching their limit.

Procedure
1. **Warm-up:** Begin with a light warm-up to prepare the body for exercise. Perform a few minutes of light cardiovascular activity, such as jogging or jumping jacks, to increase heart rate and warm up the muscles.
2. **Set up:** Find a flat and non-slippery surface to perform the push-ups. Place a mat or towel on the floor for added comfort if desired.
3. **Starting position:** Assume a prone position on the floor, facing downward. Position your hands slightly wider than shoulder-width apart, directly under your shoulders. Your toes should be in contact with the floor, legs extended, and body straight from head to heels.
4. **Execution:** Push yourself up by extending your arms fully. Then, lower your body by bending your elbows while keeping your body straight and aligned. Lower until your chest or chin touches the floor. Ensure proper form is maintained throughout the movement, with a straight line from head to heels.
5. **Test administration:** Start the test by performing continuous push-ups at a controlled pace. Lower your body until your chest or chin touches the floor and then push up until your arms are fully extended. Keep a steady rhythm and avoid pausing or resting for an extended period during the test. The test ends when you are unable to maintain proper form or complete another full push-up.
6. **Recording results:** Note the total number of push-ups completed before reaching fatigue. Make sure the number is accurately recorded for evaluation and comparison.
7. **Interpret the results:** Excellent, Very good, Good, Fair, and Poor Muscle Endurance standard charts can be found online to compare.

Chapter 7: Understanding Exercise (cont.)

Activity: Testing Your Fitness (cont.)

Cardiovascular Fitness

Instructions for Students:

The **Step Test** is a cardiovascular exercise that is very easy on the joints so most populations can perform it very easily.

Equipment Needed:
- A sturdy step or platform (about 12–16 inches high)
- Stopwatch or timer
- Heart rate monitor (optional)

Procedure
1. **Warm-up:** Begin with a light warm-up to prepare your body for exercise. You can do a few minutes of brisk walking or light jogging to increase your heart rate.
2. **Set up the step:** Position the step or platform in a stable area, ensuring it's at a height of about 12–16 inches (30–40 cm).
3. **Start the timer:** Begin the timer or stopwatch.
4. **Stepping activity:** Step up onto the platform with one foot, followed by the other foot. Step down one foot at a time, returning to the starting position. Repeat this stepping pattern at a consistent pace, maintaining a rhythm and using both feet. 
5. **Step duration:** Continue stepping for a total duration of 3 minutes. Try to maintain a steady and controlled pace throughout the test.
6. **Monitor heart rate:** After the 3-minute stepping period, immediately stop and measure your heart rate. You can use a heart rate monitor or manually take your pulse by placing two fingers on your wrist or neck and counting the beats for 15 seconds, then multiply the count by 4 to get beats per minute (bpm).
7. **Recovery:** Rest quietly for 1 minute while continuing to monitor your heart rate.
8. **Heart rate recovery:** After 1 minute of rest, measure your heart rate again. Again, you can use a heart rate monitor or manually take your pulse.
9. **Record the data:** Note both your heart rate immediately after the stepping activity and your heart rate after 1 minute of rest.
10. **Interpret the results:** Compare your heart rate recovery to established norms for your age and gender. A quicker decrease in heart rate during the recovery period is generally indicative of better cardiovascular fitness.

Chapter 7: Understanding Exercise (cont.)

Activity: Testing Your Fitness (cont.)

Flexibility Test

Instructions for Students:

The **sit-and-reach test** is the most common method used to assess flexibility. It measures the distance an individual can reach forward while sitting with legs extended.

Procedure

1. **Warm-up:** Begin with a light warm-up to prepare the body for the test. Perform a few minutes of light aerobic activity, such as jogging or cycling, to increase blood flow and warm up the muscles.
2. **Equipment setup:** Place a sit and reach box or a measuring tape on the floor. The sit and reach box typically has a ruler or measuring scale attached to it.
3. **Starting position:** Sit on the floor with legs extended straight in front of you. Your feet should be pressed against the sit and reach box or the measuring tape. Position your heels against the edge of the box or tape.
4. **Execution:** Place your hands on top of each other, with palms facing down. Keeping your knees extended, reach forward as far as possible by bending at the waist and sliding your hands along the measuring scale. Avoid forcefully bouncing or jerking during the reach. Exhale as you reach forward and hold the furthest position for a couple of seconds.
5. **Measurement:** Note the distance (in centimeters or inches) reached on the measuring scale. This measurement represents your sit and reach score.
6. **Repeated attempts:** Perform the sit and reach test three times, with a short rest period between each attempt. Record the best score out of the three trials.

Make sure to keep your legs straight throughout the test. Do not bounce or use jerky movements to reach further. Go in a slow and controlled motion.

Chapter 8: Aerobic Exercise

Aerobic exercise, also known as **cardiovascular exercise**, is defined as repetitive movement that increases your heart rate and breathing rate for an extended period of time, working slow-twitch muscle fibers. Jogging, swimming, cycling, or other forms of cardiovascular exercise all increase your heart rate and force the heart to pump faster than it normally would have to at rest. Your heart is a muscle, so the more you work it out, the stronger it gets. Your lungs also get stronger, which improves your lung function. Aerobic exercise also burns a lot of calories per hour, which helps weight management as well. In addition, aerobic exercise has huge mental health benefits, including lowering depression and anxiety.

ACSM Guidelines

The American College of Sports Medicine (ACSM) recommends the following FITT (frequency, intensity, time, and type) guidelines for aerobic exercise:

1. **Frequency:** At least 3–5 days per week
2. **Intensity:** Moderate Intensity (40–60% of maximum heart rate) to vigorous intensity (60–85% of maximum heart rate)
3. **Time:** 150 minutes per week of moderate intensity exercise OR 75 minutes of vigorous intensity exercise
4. **Type:** Any activity that uses large muscle groups and can be sustained for a prolonged period of time, such as walking, running, cycling, swimming, or dancing

This can be broken down very easily into days. Say you want to do 3 days of aerobic exercise per week and you need 150 minutes of moderate intensity cardiovascular exercise.

150 / 3 = 50 minutes of moderate activity exercise 3 days per week.

Moderate intensity means you should be able to talk and carry on a conversation, but it should be hard to talk. If it's easy to talk while you're doing it, then that is **low intensity** exercise. If you can't talk very well while exercising, it is categorized as **vigorous intensity**.

If you enjoy running at vigorous intensity, you would only need to run 75 minutes per week (since it's harder on the heart than moderate intensity exercise, you need less of it to reap the same benefits). 75 / 3 = 25 minutes. You would have to do 25 minutes of running 3 times a week to reap all of the benefits of cardiovascular exercise.

First decide how many days per week you want to do cardiovascular exercise, then decide how intense you want the exercise to be, then divide the number of minutes by the days to see how long your sessions should be.

Importance of Aerobic Exercise for Cardiorespiratory Health

Aerobic exercise, or cardiovascular exercise, improves the health of the cardiovascular system as well as the respiratory system. Your **cardiovascular system** is what pumps blood and oxygen throughout your body. Your **respiratory system** is what breathes in oxygen and breathes

Chapter 8: Aerobic Exercise (cont.)

out your body's byproduct carbon dioxide. When you run or jog, your body is burning more calories, or energy, than it normally does. To burn calories, your body needs oxygen. So, if you are burning more calories than usual, your body needs more oxygen. Your respiratory system breathes in the oxygen, then your circulatory system has to transport the oxygen to your muscles so you can continue to run or jog. Your body adapts to exercise. This is called the SAID (Specific Adaption of Imposed Demands) principle. So, if you run or jog all the time, your body begins to change in order to help you run and jog better. This is how your body gets stronger, through repeated bouts of exercise. These are the key adaptations your body will go through in order to help you get better at aerobic exercise, which also translates to a healthier body.

- **Increase in Heart Strength & Size**
  - ◆ Your heart gets stronger and bigger as you get better at aerobic exercise. Your heart pumps blood throughout the body, so when you do aerobic exercise, you are making it pump harder and faster in order to supply blood to the rest of the body. Your body responds by growing the heart muscle so it can pump stronger and faster in order to help you get better at cardiovascular exercise. This makes it more efficient at pumping blood ALL the time, which increases your health and decreases your likelihood of cardiovascular disease.

- **Lower Resting Heart Rate**
  - ◆ As your heart becomes stronger and more efficient, it doesn't need to work as hard to maintain blood flow to the body. This means your resting heart rate lowers over time. Think about it like this, the more you use something, the faster it breaks down. If your car has a ton of miles on it, it will start to break down faster than a similar car that has very few miles on it. When you aerobic train, you are making your heart beat faster for a short period of time. This makes your heart stronger and more efficient so that when you are resting, your heart doesn't have to work very hard at all. Theoretically, this means your heart will have to work less hard throughout your entire life, meaning it will take much longer to break down than someone who has a high resting heart rate and doesn't exercise.

- **Decrease in Blood Pressure**
  - ◆ Aerobic exercise increases blood flow throughout the entire body. Blood is carried by veins, arteries, and capillaries. By increasing the amount of blood in those blood vessels, the body gets better at constricting and dilating those blood vessels, as in they stay more elastic. **Dilation** means your blood vessels relax and get bigger, this lowers your blood pressure. **Constriction** means your blood vessels contract, or tighten, which raises your blood pressure. During exercise, your blood vessels constrict. By raising the blood pressure, the blood moves FASTER and can get to your muscles quicker. When you are done exercising, your blood vessels relax and slow down, or dilate, and this lowers your blood pressure. It is very bad for your blood vessels to be constricted all the time, which happens to people who don't exercise. When your blood pressure is high all the time, it wears down your body over time, and you're more likely to have a heart attack or stroke.

- **Enhanced Lung Function**
  - ◆ Because your lungs, the key organ in your respiratory system, have to work harder to take in enough oxygen to sustain your aerobic exercise session, your breathing rate increases and you take in larger volumes of air. This expands and strengthens your lungs over

Chapter 8: Aerobic Exercise (cont.)

time. This improves their capacity to take in oxygen and remove carbon dioxide. They get more efficient and better at their jobs, making your everyday life easier. When you are hiking, walking up steps, carrying groceries, etc., your body will be better at breathing so you won't be as tired with normal everyday activities. You'll be able to do fun things, like hiking, much longer in your life. If you've ever seen older adults who struggle to walk long distances without getting out of breath, these are the consequences of not training your respiratory system.

- **Increased HDL Cholesterol**
  - ◆ Regular aerobic exercise has been shown to increase **HDL**, or **high-density lipoprotein**. HDL is thought of as your "good" cholesterol. Think of your veins and arteries like a road, and think about cholesterol as cars. If you have too many cars on one road, traffic slows down. Sometimes you even have a traffic jam where no cars can move and traffic gets stuck. Well, a traffic jam in the circulatory system can lead to a heart attack or a stroke. Your HDL is like a tow truck. It actually picks up the bad or stuck cholesterol (**low-density lipoprotein**, or **LDL**) and carries it back to the liver. The tow truck takes broken down cars back to the shop to get fixed, hopefully before there is a traffic jam. HDL picks up the "stuck" pieces of cholesterol before you have a heart attack or stroke. Aerobic exercise has been found to increase the amount of HDL we have in our body, so we have plenty of tow trucks to keep our veins and arteries clear.

- **Weight Management**
  - ◆ Aerobic exercise increases the demands of energy on your body. Because running is harder than walking, you burn more calories running than you do walking. You burn a lot more calories running than you do resting. Because you are burning more calories, this increases your metabolism and helps you burn off more of the food that you eat throughout the day. This means you either get to eat a little bit more because you're burning more calories (if you want to stay the same weight), or it makes it easier to lose weight because it helps put your body in a calorie deficit, which is essential for weight loss. If your goal is to gain weight, cardiovascular exercise can make it harder because you're burning more calories, so you will have to eat more food to counteract the extra calorie burn.

Types of Aerobic Exercise
- **Running/Jogging**
  - ◆ **Pros:** Running is easy to do and very convenient. It can be done outside almost anywhere or on a treadmill, all you really need is shoes and space.
  - ◆ **Cons:** Running is high-impact and puts a lot of stress on the knees and ankles over time. When you're a healthy body weight and young, you can get away with a lot of running because your joints are still healthy and you aren't very heavy so you aren't causing a lot of blunt force trauma on your joints. If you are overweight or obese or have a history of injuries in your knees or ankles, running may not be a suitable choice because you're putting a lot more force on each of those joints with each and every step. This can lead to wear and tear and joint replacement down the road.
  - ◆ **Advice:** Do not run on the sidewalk, since they are very hard and dense and increase the pressure on your joints with each stride. You should run on the asphalt, or road, whenever it is safe to do so. It is important to always wear a light reflected vest and clothing during your runs so oncoming traffic can see you, decreasing the likelihood of getting hit.

Chapter 8: Aerobic Exercise (cont.)

- **Cycling**
  - ◆ **Pros:** Cycling is a low-impact (that means easy on the joints) exercise that provides a good cardiovascular workout. It can be done outside or indoors on a stationary bike. Bikes can also be set to increase the intensity or resistance, so many cyclers gain a significant amount of leg muscle from cycling.

  - ◆ **Cons:** Outdoor cycling may depend on weather conditions and access to safe cycling routes. Many cities don't have cycling lanes yet, which means you will often have to cycle with traffic. It is important to wear light reflected clothing so cars and traffic can see you. Also, you are going at a greater speed than running, meaning if you get in a wreck or crash, you are more likely to be injured.
  - ◆ **Advice:** Pick cycling routes with low traffic and few potholes. Avoid potholes and loose gravel, as they can cause accidents. Join a cycling club and cycle together so drivers of cars are more easily able to see all of the riders and are less likely to hit you.

- **Swimming**
  - ◆ **Pros:** Swimming is a low-impact, full body workout that is great for your cardiovascular system. It is very easy on the joints and is suitable for many different fitness levels.

  - ◆ **Cons:** Not everyone has access to a pool; some towns and cities don't have a pool at all. Skill is also required as you have to know how to swim in order to use swimming as an exercise. There is always a potential for drowning as well if something happens, like a cardiac event or even a cramp.
  - ◆ **Advice:** Swim in pools with lifeguards on duty. This will decrease the likelihood of drowning. Take swim lessons early on in life so you learn different styles of swimming. Changing the style you swim can decrease the likelihood of overuse strains as well.

- **Aerobic Dance Classes**
  - ◆ **Pros:** Dance classes have picked up in the past few years as a fun and social way to combine cardiovascular exercise with dancing movement. It can improve coordination, flexibility, as well as your cardiovascular health. The music and group atmosphere can provide more motivation than just exercising alone.
  - ◆ **Cons:** Coordination and dance skills may be required, and it may be hard to learn the chorography of the class. The class intensity can vary according to the dance, the class, and the instructor. Some people may feel self-conscious dancing in front of groups of people.
  - ◆ **Advice:** Make friends with the people in class and choose classes with dim lighting. It will take the edge off if you're friends with everyone in class. If the lighting is dim, you will care a lot less about what you're doing and enjoy the flow of the class.

Chapter 8: Aerobic Exercise (cont.)

- **Rowing**
  - ◆ **Pros:** Rowing is a great full-body workout that is low-impact. You can row competitively on a boat or use a rowing machine. Resistance can be changed to make it harder or easier, depending on your fitness level.
  - ◆ **Cons:** Rowing can be hard on your low back if done incorrectly. Even done correctly, you must be careful of overuse injuries with your low back, as it has been known to cause strains and injuries.
  - ◆ **Advice:** Find a high-quality rower that fits your body's needs. Some rowers are low to the ground and place more strain on the low back, whereas others are higher off the ground and take a lot of pressure off the back.

Choosing What Is Right for You

There are many different types of cardiovascular exercise. As with anything in life, too much of a good thing can also be a bad thing. Just like it's important to eat a variety of vegetables and protein sources to make sure you're getting all your vitamins and minerals, it is important to vary your types of cardiovascular training to avoid overuse injuries. If you run all the time, you will eventually wear down one of your joints and probably have to stop running. If you swim all the time, you might get bored and quit after several years of looking at the same pool water. Do different types of cardiovascular exercise to ensure you will never get bored of working out your heart and you will also avoid overuse injuries.

Many people break up their forms of cardio depending on the season.

Summer – Take advantage of the warm weather by swimming outdoors at your local pool. The cool pool water also does a great job at keeping your body cooler to avoid overheating.

Fall – Fall is a great time to run. It is cool and you can always dress in layers, depending on the weather. Find a road or trail that is pretty when the leaves change colors and enjoy the cool weather as your body produces most of your heat.

Winter – Winter is a great time to try indoor dance or other group fitness classes such as step aerobics or kickboxing. While the weather is too harsh to work out outside, take advantage of local group classes that take place in a heated room.

Spring – Spring is a great time to bring out your bicycle from storage. Enjoy riding as the grass begins to turn green and flowers bloom. Since the weather is more temperate in the spring, you won't have to worry about overheating as much while on the road.

You could even do different types of cardio throughout the week. You're not limited to any one type for long periods of time. Most importantly, pick something you enjoy doing. If you enjoy it, you're much more likely to continue doing it. If you don't enjoy it, find a way to make it more enjoyable. Find a running partner you enjoy talking to or a group of friends to cycle or take classes with. Working out with someone else is always much more enjoyable!

Chapter 8: Aerobic Exercise (cont.)

Key Notes

- **Aerobic exercise**, also known as **cardiovascular exercise**, is defined as repetitive movement that increases your heart rate and breathing rate for an extended period of time working slow-twitch muscle fibers. ACSM Guidelines:
  - **Frequency** – 3 to 5 days a week
  - **Intensity** – moderate to vigorous intensity
  - **Time** – 150 minutes moderate intensity or 75 minutes vigorous intensity per week
  - **Type** – activity that uses large muscle groups and can be sustained for a prolonged period of time
- **Moderate Intensity Exercise:** Exercise that elevates the heart rate and breathing rate, but still allows you to carry on a conversation comfortably
- **Vigorous Intensity Exercise:** Exercise that significantly increases your heart rate and breathing rate, so much so that it is typically very challenging to have a conversation while exercising
- **Benefits of Aerobic Exercise:**
  - **Increase in Heart Strength & Size**
  - **Lower Resting Heart Rate**
  - **Decrease in Blood Pressure**
  - **Enhanced Lung Function**
  - **Increased HDL Cholesterol**
  - **Weight Management**
- **Types of Aerobic Exercise:**
  - **Running/Jogging**
  - **Cycling**
  - **Swimming**
  - **Aerobic Dance Classes**
  - **Rowing**

Chapter 8: Aerobic Exercise (cont.)

Activity : Cardiovascular Exercise at Home

Instructions for Teachers: Because everyone has different likes and dislikes when it comes to exercise, it's important for teens to find what they like doing. The best exercise is the exercise people will stick with, and forcing someone to run who prefers to bike or dance will only make them hate exercise. For this reason, it's important that the take-home message is to find something that gets your heart rate up that you enjoy, and do it several times a week. ACSM Guidelines advocate for 75 minutes of vigorous activity per week. For this activity, if they are able, assign the students to perform 75 minutes of vigorous activity divided up into however many days they want. Encourage them to try different things such as cycling, rowing, swimming, jogging, or following dancing videos or HIIT workouts online. They can do whatever they want, but they have to keep their heart rate up to Vigorous Target Heart Rate Zone, which can be found here. Have the students find their own heart rate zone using these calculations, and encourage them to do the whole 75 minutes that week. Have them write down their thoughts AFTER the cardiovascular session is completed. Usually they will be in much better moods and have almost euphoric energy afterwards.

During vigorous activity, the heart rate typically increases significantly. The heart rate percentage during vigorous activity can vary depending on an individual's age, fitness level, and **maximum heart rate** (MHR). A common method to estimate the target heart rate range for vigorous activity is to calculate a percentage of the maximum heart rate. The maximum heart rate can be estimated using the formula: Maximum Heart Rate (MHR) = 220 - Age. For vigorous activity, the target heart rate is typically around 70–85% of the maximum heart rate.

Here's an example of calculating the target heart rate of a 16-year-old individual:

1. Calculate the maximum heart rate (MHR):
    - MHR = 220 - Age
    - MHR = 220 - 16
    - MHR = 204 beats per minute (bpm)
2. Determine the Target Heart Rate Range for vigorous activity:
    - Lower Range: 70% of MHR
    - Lower Range = 0.7 * 204
    - Lower Range = 142.8 or 143
    - Upper Range: 85% of MHR
    - Upper Range = 0.85 * 204
    - Upper Range = 173.4 or 174
3. So, for a 16-year-old, the goal will to be to keep the heart rate between 143–174 beats per minute. This can be measured with a smart watch or heart rate monitor or by periodically checking your pulse and counting your beats per minute for 60 seconds.

If the student isn't able to check their heart rate, a good rule of thumb for measuring vigorous activity is "The Talk Test." Students should be able to say 1 or 2 words while performing the exercise but not be able to complete full sentences and carry on a conversation well during exercise. That's how you know if you're in the vigorous zone.

Chapter 9: Anaerobic Exercise

Anaerobic exercise, or resistance training, involves short bursts of intense activity at very high intensities that target fast-twitch muscle fibers, which generate quick and powerful contractions. Resistance training helps build strength, power, muscle mass, and bone density. Resistance training also makes your metabolism faster, makes day-to-day life easier (carrying groceries, climbing stairs), improves insulin sensitivity, enhances cardiovascular health, improves mood and reduces symptoms of depression and anxiety, prevents injuries, and helps improve memory, attention, and other executive functions.

ACSM Guidelines

ACSM recommends the following FITT guidelines for resistance training:

1. **Frequency:** Each major muscle group should be trained 2–3 days per week.
2. **Intensity:** 60%–70% of 1 rep max for beginners and intermediate exercises. You can gradually increase to percentages at or above 80% as experience is gained. This means repetitions should be hard enough that you can only get between 6–15 repetitions. If you can get more than 15 repetitions, it is too light.
3. **Time:** No specific duration of training has been defined, but usually strength training sessions take between 45 minutes to 1 hour and 15 minutes. Rest in between sets should take 2–4 minutes.
4. **Type:** Resistance exercising involving each major muscle group, or motor pattern, are recommended. The beginning of the session should focus on multi-joint exercises, and towards the end of the session, single-joint exercises may be utilized.

Resistance training at its core follows a principle known as **progressive overload**. Progressive overload simply means if you want to continue making yourself more physically fit, you must continue to make the exercises harder in some way. If you think about it, this makes a lot of sense. If you can bench press 45 pounds and you get a little stronger afterwards, then the next time you bench 45 pounds, it will be too light for your muscles because now that they are a little stronger, they should be benching 55 pounds. After each weightlifting session, assuming you  get enough sleep and protein, you should be 1–2% stronger. This means you will have to continually make the exercise harder in order to make the same improvements. We will discuss the ways to achieve progressive overload later in the book, but please note this is the most important principle in continually improving your physical fitness.

Importance of Anaerobic Resistance Training

Anaerobic training is incredibly important to maintain and improve overall health and fitness. For thousands of years, we lived very active lifestyles and performed very hard jobs all day long. Now, due to technological advancements, most of our days are very sedentary and not physically demanding. This has led to a major decline in our overall health, as you can see by the many diseases that are now plaguing our society. Strength training has taken the forefront of exercise to counteract this sedentary lifestyle. We have found that we can reap the same benefits of living very active lifestyles (like we have in the past) by resistance training for 45–75 minutes most days per week. Resistance training places much more load on your muscles than you have to do in your

Chapter 9: Anaerobic Exercise (cont.)

normal daily activities. This short burst of intense work has a ton of benefits throughout the body that will help you stay physically fit without having to work hard all day. Here are some of the major benefits of resistance training. For the purpose of this book, strength training, anaerobic training, and resistance training are all used interchangeably.

- **Increased Muscle Mass and Strength**
  - ◆ By applying a great deal of stress to the muscles, your muscles respond by growing in order to prepare for the next bout of exercise. Just like your heart gets bigger and stronger with cardiovascular exercise, so too do your muscles respond by getting bigger and stronger. Larger muscles produce more force, and you become stronger with everyday movements. Muscles also are used to store sugar, so the more muscle you have, the better your insulin sensitivity is likely to be, making you less likely to get type 2 diabetes. Strength is also essential for performing daily activities such as walking up steps, moving furniture, carrying groceries, maintaining proper posture, and reducing the risk of injuries. There is a saying that "weak things break," and you want your body to be as strong as it can be so it's less likely to break.
- **Increased Metabolic Rate/Metabolism**
  - ◆ Resistance training increases the metabolism both during exercise and after exercise. Cardiovascular exercise only burns calories during exercise. Resistance training burns calories during exercise, and also burns calories repairing tissue after exercise. When your body is trying to repair your muscles to make them grow back stronger, they need calories to use as fuel to actually build the muscle back. This means your metabolism is on "high" all the time. This is great for lower body fat levels over time.
- **Improved Bone Health**
  - ◆ Just like your muscles, your bones get stronger with resistance training. When performing a squat or jump, you are placing more weight on your bones than usual. **Wolf's Law of Bone Remodeling** is a biological law that states your bones adapt and get stronger when stress is applied to them. This makes you less likely to break any bones.
- **Improved Tendon and Ligament Health**
  - ◆ Much like Wolf's Law, **Davis's Law** is a biological law that states soft tissue, such as your tendons and ligaments, gets stronger through resistance training. Counter to popular belief, your joints should get stronger if you're lifting correctly and progressing safely.
- **Increased Joint Stability and Function**
  - ◆ Resistance training through full range of motion has actually been shown to be just as good for flexibility as actual flexibility training and also improves your body's ability to control the joint during movement. When working out in a full range of motion, you are essentially stretching your muscles and joints, except you are doing it with MORE weight, making it a great way to improve flexibility and stability.
- **Hormonal Benefits**
  - ◆ Resistance training triggers the release of human growth hormone and testosterone, which helps muscles grow and repair, burns body fat, and is overall good for the body. When your testosterone increases, so does your estrogen to keep in balance. This is good for your joints and helps you stay healthy over time.

Chapter 9: Anaerobic Exercise (cont.)

As you can see, resistance training has a ton of benefits for the body. It is important to note that although there are so many benefits, there is also a lot of risk. Most people know how to run or ride a bike. You don't have to worry about form as much because those forms of exercise are relatively safe. Learning how to squat or bench press correctly is much harder. Most of the people who get hurt through resistance training exercise simply were never taught correctly how to perform the exercises to avoid injury. There are so many exercises, it is hard to learn to do them all correctly. This is why it is so important to find a good coach or guide who can show you how to do the exercises properly while you are young. That way you can avoid injuries and risks down the road. Personal trainers, strength and conditioning coaches, and physical therapists can all be useful guides to teaching you how to perform the exercises safely.

Types of Resistance Training

- **Bodyweight Resistance Training/Calisthenics** – Bodyweight training is a form of resistance training that uses your own body as resistance.

  - **Pros:** Bodyweight exercise can be done anywhere and requires little to no equipment. It is great for beginners to learn movements such as air squats, pushups, pullups, and planks. It promotes strength gains, muscle gains, and improves coordination. It is also very suitable for different fitness levels, and there are many exercise modifications if an exercise is too hard. You can add resistance bands to the routine to increase the intensity of the exercises. There is also a low risk of injury since you are only using your body as resistance.
  - **Cons:** Eventually bodyweight exercises will stop improving your physical fitness. Since you are only using your body as resistance, it is hard to increase the resistance over time. Remember the principle of progressive overload—you have to make things harder over time in order to continue to get more fit. It is hard to make pushups harder, so while bodyweight training is great for beginners, it is less suitable for intermediate or advanced exercisers.

- **Machine-Based Resistance Training** – Machine-based training is commonly found in home gyms and commercial gyms. The machine controls the weight and there are different machines for each body group. For example, a leg extension machine ONLY extends your leg. A chest press machine ONLY works your chest. You need a different machine for each and every muscle group.

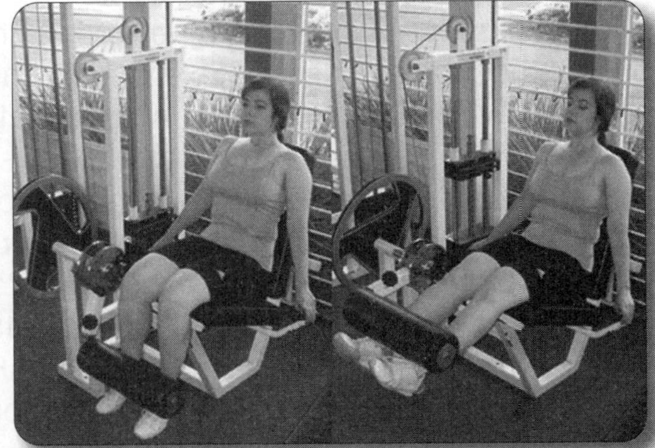

  - **Pros:** Machines provide a guided range of motion so you don't have to work your stabilizer muscles, this makes them very easy to use for beginners. They also isolate individual muscle groups, so if you want to JUST make your chest bigger, you can do only a chest press exercise to work on that area. Machines also can move up and move down

Chapter 9: Anaerobic Exercise (cont.)

in weight so you can progressively add weight as you go, ensuring you will always be able to progressively overload the muscles and continue to grow healthier.

♦ **Cons:** Since the machine is guiding the movement, you don't get better at controlling the weight yourself. You do not get more athletic and you do not get better at moving with machines, as they simply work the muscles. There are also smaller muscles in the body than the machines can target, specifically the low back. This means some of these muscles will be underdeveloped and more likely to get injured during day-to-day activity. You also need to have a gym that has access to all the different machines, which is hard to find in some areas.

● **Free-Weight Resistance Training** – Free-weight training carries the most risk but also carries the most reward with exercise. This works your cardiovascular system, stabilizer muscles, strength, stability, improves athleticism, and makes you better at moving in everyday life. Free weights focus on **movement patterns** such as pushing exercises, pulling exercises, squatting exercises, hip hinging exercises, and lunging exercises.

♦ **Pros:** Every exercise is nearly a full-body exercise, meaning you work a lot of muscle groups very quickly. Your progress will be the fastest with free weights, and you will also get better at moving and improve athletic performance. Weight can be increased very slowly by adding 2.5–5-pound increments over time. Generally, you just need dumbbells, a bar, weight plates, a bench, and a squat rack, and you can do hundreds of free weight movements. You may be able to use household items such as canned foods or jugs of water to do some of the exercises at home.

♦ **Cons:** Using free weights requires proper form and technique to minimize the risk of injury. Beginners will need guidance to learn proper lifting techniques and to build strong habits early on in their exercise careers. Some exercises, like the power clean, have greater risk than others, like the squat.

● **CrossFit** – CrossFit is a newer form of resistance training that attempts to combine many of the benefits of aerobic exercises with anaerobic exercise training.

♦ **Pros:** CrossFit offers a combination of strength training, cardiovascular exercise, and other functional movements. It is typically done in groups and provides a community atmosphere, which is highly supportive. You generally burn quite a few calories during workouts because they are so hard.

♦ **Cons:** Because the exercises are hard to learn AND intense, the risk of injury is high with CrossFit if proper form and technique are not prioritized. It may not be suitable for beginners because of this. CrossFit facilities are also typically costly, and you must find qualified trainers to make your workouts.

● **Powerlifting** – Powerlifting is a strength sport focusing on bench press, barbell squat, and the deadlift. The goal of a powerlifter is to get as strong as possible in these three exercises.

♦ **Pros:** The bench, squat, and deadlift work a wide variety of muscles so only getting good at these three exercises will result in a lot of muscle mass and carry over strength in other

Chapter 9: Anaerobic Exercise (cont.)

areas of your life. Powerlifting can be a great complement to an athletic program if used properly.

◆ **Cons:** By only focusing on three major lifts, the likelihood of overuse injuries is high. Powerlifting also doesn't typically focus on any muscular endurance exercises since the goal is JUST strength. Strength is only one of the five components of physical fitness, so you are losing out on the other four components if all you do is powerlift.

● **Bodybuilding** – Bodybuilding was the first form of resistance training to really popularize lifting weights. The focus is on making muscles as big as possible, sometimes focusing on smaller muscle groups, like the shoulders, to make people appear larger.

◆ **Pros:** Bodybuilders typically use many isolation movements and machines. This is a very safe way to exercise to avoid injuries.

◆ **Cons:** Because the focus is on how you look and how big your muscles are, bodybuilders usually avoid functional strength training exercises that help improve athleticism and coordination. Also, making your muscles too big eventually gets in the way of everyday life and causes strain on your heart as you are now walking around carrying a lot of excess muscle mass.

A balanced approach to all of these various forms of exercise is known as functional training. **Functional training** involves primarily free weight exercises focusing on the major **movement patterns**: **pushing, pulling, squatting, hip hinging,** and **lunging**. Along with these free weight exercises, you can use machines and bodyweight exercises at the end of your workouts to work on individual body parts. Generally, functional training will consist of a dynamic warmup with bodyweight exercises, free weight strength training, and end with isolation movements at the end of the workout. This covers muscular endurance, muscular strength, and some flexibility and cardiovascular exercise, and helps keep your body fat percentage low. To avoid injury, you want to do a mix between all these forms of exercise. Beginners may want to stick with bodyweight and machine-based exercises until they find a reputable coach or trainer to teach them how to use free weights properly. From there, they should focus on movement patterns to build a base of physical fitness. As they gain experience with these exercises, they can then differentiate between their sports, powerlifting, bodybuilding, or CrossFit, or just keep lifting for general health and wellness.

Movement Patterns & Examples

Movement pattern resistance training focuses on **multi-joint exercises**. Multi-joint means that multiple joints are moving and contracting at one time. A single-joint exercise involves only one joint moving at a time, like a bicep curl that only moves your elbow. Multi-joint works multiple joints, so a barbell row that involves your shoulders and your elbows moving works multiple sets of muscles instead of just one muscle. For example, a leg extension isolates the quad since the only joint being moved is your knee. A squat involves moving the hip joint, the knee joint, and the ankle joint, making it work your hips, quads and hamstrings, and calves. When choosing exercises, it is the most time-efficient to choose multi-joint exercises because they work so many different muscle

Chapter 9: Anaerobic Exercise (cont.)

groups at once. By working more than one joint, you are working multiple muscle groups with one exercise. You are building more real-life strength, power, muscle mass, coordination, stamina, and endurance. When you are working out with single-joint exercises, like a bicep curl, you are working one small muscle group. These multi-joint exercises are broken down into different movement patterns. **Movement patterns** are the brain's basic "computer programs" for how to move and move well. These are things we naturally do every day whether we realize it or not. We squat, hip hinge, push, pull, and lunge every day. These are all multi-joint movements that work all of the muscles in the body. So when we are exercising, we should train these movement patterns by adding resistance to them. This will help us work all of the muscles in our body and make us better at moving and sports in general. There are five major movement patterns, and we will provide exercise progressions, beginning with bodyweight, for them all.

1. **Push** – We push things away from us every day: pushing doors open, pushing shopping carts, pushing furniture across the room. Anything that involves taking an object and moving it farther away from your body is characterized as a pushing movement. Pushing movements primarily work the chest, triceps, and shoulders all at one time, making them great multi-joint exercises that work multiple muscle groups.
   a. Incline Pushups
   b. Pushup
   c. Dumbbell Bench Press
   d. Dumbbell Overhead Press
   e. Landmine Press
   f. Barbell Overhead Press
   g. Barbell Bench Press
2. **Pull** – Pulling movements involve pulling things toward your body. They are the opposite of the pushing muscle groups. Pulling a door toward you, pulling luggage, and pulling yourself up on a set of monkey bars, are all examples of pulling motions you would do throughout the day. Physical labor jobs are full of pulling motions using wrenches or other tools. Pulling movements work the shoulders, back muscles, and biceps.
   a. Inverted Row
   b. Lat Pulldown
   c. Row Machine
   d. DB Chest Supported Row
   e. Chin-up
   f. Pull-up
   g. Barbell Bent Over Row
3. **Squat** – Squatting involves bending the knees and hips. We do this the most every single day, every time we get off of a chair and stand up, we are practicing squatting. We do this hundreds of times throughout the day. Squatting works your entire core, quads, hamstrings, glutes, and calves and is one of the best exercises for your brain. Getting a stronger squat in the gym will help build all of your leg muscles and carry over to jumping higher and running faster.

Chapter 9: Anaerobic Exercise (cont.)

   a. Bodyweight Squat
   b. Goblet Box Squat
   c. Goblet Squat
   d. Front Box Squat
   e. Front Squat
   f. Barbell Box Squat
   g. Barbell Squat

4. **Hip Hinge –** Hip hinging involves bending over from the hips, while maintaining a flat back, and usually picking something up. When lifting objects from the ground, putting your shoes on, or picking up laundry baskets, usually this is done by shooting your hips back and picking up the objects from the ground. This works your entire back, hips, and hamstrings and makes you very strong and resilient to back and hamstring injuries, which are common in some sports.
   a. Glute Bridge
   b. Hip Thrust
   c. Barbell Glute Bridge
   d. Barbell Hip Thrust
   e. Kettlebell Deadlift
   f. Trap Bar Deadlift
   g. Barbell Deadlift

5. **Lunge –** Lunging or stepping up is a single leg movement that we also do hundreds of times a day. Walking up steps, getting out of a car, trying to catch your balance, stopping to tie your shoe, hiking, and anything that involves balancing on one leg for a brief moment of time is characterized as a lunge movement pattern. Lunging works your quads, hamstrings, and glutes very well and also improves balance and coordination, making it a staple for athletes and for older adults who want to improve their balance.
   a. Split Squat
   b. Step Up
   c. Reverse Lunge
   d. Forward Lunge
   e. Lateral Lunge
   f. Bulgarian Split Squat

Load, Reps, Sets, Rest

Load is based on a percentage of your one rep max. **One rep max** means the most amount of weight you can do with an exercise (with good form) for one rep. You will then use that one rep to calculate the percentages you will work out with. Higher percentages mean heavier lifting and more of a focus on strength, whereas lower percentages mean more reps and the emphasis is placed on muscular endurance. **Reps**, or repetitions, means how many times you will perform the exercise at one given time. **Sets** is how many times you'll perform your prescribed repetitions. So, 3 sets of 10 repetitions means you will do something 10 times back to back followed by a brief

Chapter 9: Anaerobic Exercise (cont.)

rest, then do it another 10 times back to back, a brief rest, then you will complete them another 10 times. That is 3 x 10 or 3 sets of 10 repetitions. **Rest** varies greatly depending on your goals, but that is the time you wait in between doing another set. Rest time is very important. If you don't wait long enough, you won't be able to go heavy enough to grow muscle and get stronger, and if you wait too long, your muscles will get "cold," and it will be harder to perform your sets.

	Strength	Power	Muscle Mass	Endurance
Load (% of 1RM)	85–95%	60–70%	60–85%	40–60%
Reps per Set	1–5	1–5	6–12	12+
Sets per Exercise	4–7	3–5	3–8	2–4
Rest In-between Sets	3–6 Minutes	3–6 Minutes	2–5 Minutes	1–2 Minutes

Strength

To work on strength, you are lifting a very high percentage of your 1RM and taking long breaks in between each set. Your body needs this rest to recover in order for you to do your next set, so make sure you are taking adequate rest in between sets. You will gain some muscle mass, but you will primarily gain strength.

Power

Power is similar to strength in that you are doing very low reps and taking long breaks in between each set. However, you are lifting much lighter weights. The focus with power training is to use light weights but to do them very fast. This will help you jump higher and become more explosive. You will not gain very much muscle by power training, but you will get very explosive and a little bit stronger.

Muscle Mass

Bodybuilders primarily focus on this rep range and rest. You will gain the maximal amount of muscle but not get as strong or as powerful as someone focusing on those components of exercise. You must take adequate rest in between sets or you won't be able to get all your reps in the next set.

Endurance

Endurance is primarily used by endurance athletes or older adults who want to minimize risk but still improve components of their health. You can do upwards of 30–40 repetitions per set, and breaks are typically much shorter.

Chapter 9: Anaerobic Exercise (cont.)

Key Notes

- **Anaerobic exercise**, or resistance training, involves short bursts of intense activity at very high intensities that target fast-twitch muscle fibers, which generate quick and powerful contractions. ACSM Guidelines:
  - **Frequency** – train each major muscle group 2–3 days per week
  - **Intensity** – 60–70% 1RM for beginner and intermediate; 80% 1RM for experienced
  - **Time** – usually 45–75 minutes with 2–4 minutes of rest between sets
  - **Type** – resistance exercises involving each major muscle group, or motor pattern; multi-joint and single-joint exercises
- **Importance of Anaerobic Exercise/Resistance Training**
  - **Increased Muscle Mass and Strength**
  - **Increased Metabolic Rate/Metabolism**
  - **Improved Bone Health**
    - ❏ **Wolf's Law**
  - **Improved Tendon and Ligament Health**
    - ❏ **Davis's Law**
  - **Increased Joint Stability and Function**
  - **Hormonal Benefits**
- **Types of Resistance Training**
  - **Bodyweight Training/Calisthenics**
  - **Machine-Based Training**
  - **Free-Weight Resistance Training**
  - **CrossFit**
  - **Powerlifting**
  - **Bodybuilding**
- **Movement Patterns**
  - **Push**
  - **Pull**
  - **Squat**
  - **Hip Hinge**
  - **Lunge**
- **Load, Repetitions, Sets, and Rest**
  - **Strength**
  - **Power**
  - **Muscle Mass**
  - **Endurance**

Chapter 9: Anaerobic Exercise (cont.)

Activity: At-Home Resistance Training

Instructions for Students: The author of this book recognizes that not everyone will have access to a gym with free weights or exercise machines, but everyone has access to their own body and can make great progress strength training at home using bodyweight exercises. Pick out the bodyweight exercises from each of the movement patterns listed throughout the section. These will be your exercises for your workouts this week.

**Note: You should consult a doctor and your parents before starting a workout program.

1. **Push:** Incline Pushups/Pushups
2. **Pull:** Inverted Row/Pullups/Chinups
3. **Squat:** Bodyweight Air Squats
4. **Hip Hinge:** Glute Bridges/Couch Hip Thrusts
5. **Lunge:** Bodyweight Split Squat/Reverse Lunge/Step Up/Forward Lunge

Pick one exercise from each category. Because you can't add resistance/weight to the exercise to make it harder when performing bodyweight exercises, the best way to do them is to go until failure with each exercise before moving on to the next. Failure is defined as when your muscles give out and you are unable to do any more repetitions with good form. You will want to perform 2–4 rounds of each set of exercises 3 times per week, preferably every other day. You can mix and match exercises throughout the week as well.

Example:

Monday – 3 Rounds of Max Repetitions:
1. Incline Pushups
2. Inverted Row
3. Chair Squats
4. Glute Bridges
5. Split Squats

Wednesday – 3 Rounds of Max Repetitions:
1. Pushups
2. Pullups
3. Air Squats
4. Couch Hip Thrusts
5. Reverse Lunge

Friday – 3 Rounds of Max Repetitions:
1. Closegrip Pushups
2. Chinups
3. Single-Leg Squat
4. Single-Leg Couch Hip Thrust
5. Step Ups

Record how many reps you can perform of each set. The goal is to beat your old high score each week, so if you get 30 pushups per round the first week, try to get 32 pushups per round the second week. This follows the principle of **progressive overload**, which states that exercise has to get harder as you get stronger. By doing more reps or rounds each week, you will gradually continue to improve your physical fitness. Create your own workout for three days this week following these guidelines and perform them with one day of rest in between. Record how much easier the exercises get by the end of the week as you get stronger.

Chapter 10: Flexibility Training

Flexibility refers to the ability of a joint or group of joints to move through a full range of motion. Maintaining flexibility throughout life is incredibly important to your physical fitness and health because it encompasses the ability to bend, stretch, and twist joints and muscles without limitations or injury. If your muscles are flexible and you stretch them for kicking a football, you probably won't tear any of your muscles. If your muscles are tight and you try to kick a football, you will increase your likelihood of tearing your muscles because you are trying to stretch them beyond their limits. Flexibility can decrease your risk of injuries and chronic pain, promote relaxation, and is even good for the circulatory system. It can also reduce muscle soreness, improve resistance training mobility, enhance athletic performance, and improve your posture.

ACSM Guidelines

ACSM Recommends the following FITT guidelines for flexibility training:

1. **Frequency:** More than 2–3 days per week with daily being the most effective
2. **Intensity:** Stretch to the point of feeling tightness or slight discomfort.
3. **Time:** Holding a static stretch for 10–30 seconds is recommended for most adults.
4. **Type:** Static stretching (active and passive) and dynamic stretching

Static stretching refers to holding a stretch for a certain amount of time without any movement. It is what people normally think of when they think of stretching. If I asked you to touch your toes and hold a hamstring stretch for 30 seconds, that would be an example of static stretching. **Dynamic stretching** is stretching that involves active movement through a full range of motion. It requires movement, muscle activation, and coordination. Dynamic stretching is usually done in a warm-up manner like doing high knee light jogs at the beginning of practice, stretching your hip and knees through movement. Dynamic stretching should be done BEFORE your exercise session, and static stretching should be done AFTER your exercise session is completed. Dynamic stretching warms up your muscles so they can bend more easily, then static stretching is easier  because your muscles are already warm. Think about it like this. When pulling a new piece of gum, you can rip it apart accidentally. If you warm up the piece of gum and add some liquid to it (by chewing it) and then try to stretch it, you'll find that you can stretch that piece of gum very far without ripping it apart. Your muscles are the same way!

Benefits of Stretching

There are many benefits of stretching that range from relaxation and relieving tension, all the way to improving athletic performance. Muscle tightness is controlled by your brain, or your nervous system. When you stretch muscles, you're sending signals to your brain telling your brain

Chapter 10: Flexibility Training (cont.)

to "relax" that muscle. So, through regular stretching, you're calming down your nervous system and relieving tension everywhere. This has many other benefits as well.

- **Improved Flexibility and Range of Motion**
  - ◆ By signaling the muscle to relax, you can lengthen and elongate the muscle past its normal range of motion. This allows you to move more easily and with less tension, and lets your joint work through its full range of motion. This helps athletes, dancers, and other individuals who need more range of motion in order to perform their activities.
- **Enhanced Muscle Performance**
  - ◆ Dynamic stretching before exercise helps increase blood flow to the muscles, which warms them up and improves elasticity. Warm muscles are strong muscles, and more elastic muscles are "springier" so you can jump higher and run faster.
- **Injury Prevention**
  - ◆ By improving flexibility and joint mobility, tendons and muscles are less likely to strain or overexert themselves, decreasing the likelihood of muscle tears, sprains, and other injuries.
- **Enhanced Blood Circulation**
  - ◆ Stretching the muscles also stretches the blood vessels—veins and arteries—found within the muscles. This has been found to be good for the circulatory system, including circulation and nutrient delivery.
- **Stress Relief and Relaxation**
  - ◆ Stretching involves deep diaphragmatic breathing and mindfulness. Breathing deeply through your nose tells your body to calm down, relax, and unwind. It reduces tension, promotes calmness, and alleviates stress.
- **Enhances Recovery After Exercise**
  - ◆ Because exercise is very excitatory, spending time cooling down and stretching helps calm down your mind and body from the exercise. This helps relax you and puts your body in a better state to begin recovering from the exercise bout.

Types of Stretching

There are two core types of stretching, static stretching and dynamic stretching. Within static stretching, there are two subcategories called **passive stretching** and **active stretching**. It is important to understand each type, the benefits, and when to use them in your workout regimen.

- **Dynamic Stretching**
  - ◆ Involves moving parts of the body through full range of motion in a controlled manner. These movements are usually sporting specific and mimic the activities you're about to perform, like high knees before a sprint. Dynamic stretching warms up the muscles, increases blood flow, and prepares the body for movement by improving mobility and neuromuscular coordination.
  - ◆ Dynamic stretching should always be done prior to cardiovascular or resistance training exercise.
- **Static Stretching**
  - ◆ Static stretching is when you hold a particular stretch in a stationary pose for a prolonged period of time. Generally, 10–30 seconds is enough to fully relax the muscle being stretched. There are two types of static stretching, active and passive.

Chapter 10: Flexibility Training (cont.)

◆ Because muscles stretch the best when they are warm and stretching promotes relaxation in the muscles, you should always static stretch at the END of your cardiovascular or resistance training workout.

❏ **Active Stretching**

○ Active stretching is using the force of your own muscles to stretch out a muscle. This is done by yourself. For instance, to stretch your hamstrings, you would flex your quadricep muscles as hard as you can. This creates a stretching sensation in your hamstrings by flexing the opposing muscle group. 

❏ **Passive Stretching**

○ Passive stretching involves a partner, gravity, or a prop. It is when you use an external force to help apply pressure to deepen the stretch. Physical therapists will use this technique to help patients stretch beyond their normal limits.

Popular Stretching Methodologies

Yoga and Pilates are both very popular forms of flexibility training that also improve strength, balance, and overall wellbeing. While stretching can be done anywhere, there are many entire classes devoted to flexibility training, yoga and Pilates being the two main classes.

Yoga

Yoga is an ancient practice developed in India that encompasses physical postures, breath control, meditation, and many philosophical teachings. Many of the yoga positions are thought to combine physical movement and breath awareness, and help align the mind, body, and soul. There are many benefits to yoga, such as:

● **Improved flexibility** by stretching and lengthening of the muscles and connective tissues. 

● **Strength and muscle tone** by requiring a great deal of strength in different yoga poses, using many different muscle groups and stabilizer muscles.

● **Stress reducing and relaxing** by deep breathing, mindfulness, and promoting calmness and reducing stress levels.

● **Balance and stability** improvements because many yoga poses challenge the stabilizer muscles holding balance and improving **proprioception**, the awareness of the position and movement of the body.

● **Enhanced mind-body connection.** Through integrating breath, movement, and mental focus, you become better aware of your body and build self-awareness.

● **Improved posture and alignment.** By stretching tight muscles and contracting weak muscles, the body can help correct muscle imbalances and promote better alignment.

Chapter 10: Flexibility Training (cont.)

Pilates

Pilates is a low-impact exercise method that focuses on developing core strength, improving posture, and enhancing body awareness. It is typically done on a mat or a reformer machine and uses controlled movements through their full range of motion and mindful breathing. By targeting the deep stabilizer muscles of the core, back, hips, and glutes, the body stays aligned better and flexibility is improved. There are many benefits of Pilates, such as:

- **Improved flexibility** via incorporating stretching movements that help increase mobility and flexibility
- **Core strength and stability** by targeting the core muscles, which include deep abdominal and back muscles. This promotes strength, stability, and improves posture.
- **Enhanced body awareness.** By holding your body in proper alignment and building endurance in those positions and focusing on mindful movement, a better mind-body connection is made.
- **Muscle tone.** By holding many of the positions, muscles must flex and use their own weight against themselves. This is similar to bodyweight training and helps tone up muscles.
- **Improved posture and alignment.** Similar to yoga, Pilates helps to correct muscle imbalances that worsen posture over time.
- **Injury prevention and rehabilitation.** Many physical therapists use Pilates and reformer machines to rehabilitate and target damaged muscles to help recover from injury.

Key Notes

- **Flexibility** refers to the ability of a joint or group of joints to move through a full range of motion. ACSM Guidelines:
  - **Frequency** – more than 2–3 days a week; daily is most effective
  - **Intensity** – stretch to point of tightness or slight discomfort
  - **Time** – 10–30 seconds static stretch
  - **Type** – static stretching (active and passive) and dynamic stretching
- **Benefits of Stretching**
  - **Improved flexibility and range of motion**
  - **Enhanced muscle performance**
  - **Injury prevention**
  - **Enhanced blood circulation**
  - **Stress relief and relaxation**
  - **Enhances recovery after exercise**
- **Types of Stretching**
  - **Dynamic stretching**
  - **Static stretching**
    - ❑ **Active stretching**
    - ❑ **Passive stretching**
- **Popular Stretching Methodologies**
  - **Yoga**
  - **Pilates**

Chapter 10: Flexibility Training (cont.)

Activity: Practicing Mindful Yoga Movements

Instructions for Teacher: Have students perform these movements, practicing in class, then do one more time throughout the week whenever they're feeling the most stress or anxiety. Have them record how the exercises made them feel and if their anxiety and stress went down afterwards.

Instructions for Students: There are 10 foundational yoga movements that build flexibility and promote relaxation. Spend 60 seconds in each of these yoga poses, which focus on flexibility, alignment, grounding, posture improvements, and strengthening the core. Look up these poses online to see pictures or videos of how to perform each pose.

While spending 60 seconds in each pose, focus on deep long rhythmic breathing. This yoga workout should only take 10–15 minutes and can be done throughout the day whenever you're feeling the most stressed. After completing the poses, record how the exercises made you feel and if your anxiety and stress went down.

1. **Mountain Pose** *(Tadasana)*: This is a foundational standing pose that focuses on alignment, grounding, and posture.
2. **Downward-Facing Dog** *(Adho Mukha Svanasana)*: This is an invigorating pose that stretches the whole body, particularly the hamstrings, shoulders, and back. It is often included in Sun Salutations and transition sequences.
3. **Warrior Poses** *(Virabhadrasana I, II, III)*: These powerful standing poses build strength, stability, and focus. They are often practiced to develop strength in the legs and core.
4. **Tree Pose** *(Vrikshasana)*: This balancing pose promotes stability, concentration, and body awareness. It involves standing on one leg with the other foot resting on the opposite inner thigh or calf.
5. **Child's Pose** *(Balasana)*: A gentle resting pose that stretches the lower back, hips, and shoulders. It is often used as a resting position between more intense poses or as a calming posture to center oneself.
6. **Bridge Pose** *(Setu Bandhasana)*: This backbend pose strengthens the back, glutes, and legs while opening the chest and shoulders. It can be modified for different levels of flexibility.
7. **Triangle Pose** *(Trikonasana)*: This standing pose stretches the legs, opens the hips and shoulders, and strengthens the core. It is often included in sequences focusing on balance and stability.
8. **Cobra Pose** *(Bhujangasana)*: A gentle backbend that strengthens the spine, stretches the chest, and promotes flexibility in the front body. It is often practiced in sequences for spinal health and opening the heart.
9. **Seated Forward Bend** *(Paschimottanasana)*: A seated pose that stretches the back of the body, particularly the hamstrings and lower back. It promotes relaxation and flexibility.
10. **Corpse Pose** *(Savasana)*: The final relaxation pose that involves lying flat on your back, fully relaxed. It allows the body and mind to integrate the benefits of the practice and promotes deep relaxation.

Sleep

Chapter 11: Introduction to Sleep

Sleep is the third pillar of health, along with nutrition and exercise. We spend one-third of our entire life asleep. It should go without saying how important it is to do it right. Sleep is more than just your body's down time. Sleep at its essence is when your body recovers from all the strain you put yourself through during the day. All of your organs, including your brain and your muscles, need recovery every day in order to sustain themselves. While you sleep, your brain gets to work creating and storing all the memories you made that day while your muscles get to work repairing themselves from all the exercise you did that day. Your heart, veins, and circulatory system all slow down and recover from your busy day. Your body breaks itself down bit by bit every single day, then uses its sleep to recover and build itself back up stronger. Lack of sleep is so harmful to your health. It has been shown to increase your risk of obesity, diabetes, cardiovascular disease, depression, anxiety, infection, and a worsening immune system.

Basic Definition and Understanding of Sleep

Sleep is a naturally recurring state of reduced consciousness and physical activity in which a person's body and mind rest and regenerate. It is an essential physiological process that allows the body to recover, repair tissues, form memories, and reset from a long day's worth of activity.

With insufficient sleep, your body can't repair from strenuous exercise, making all the hard workouts and practices nearly worthless as your body simply doesn't have enough time to recover. With insufficient sleep, your brain can't consolidate information and form memories from the previous day. This means it's much harder to retain information from your school work and reading.

Mental health requires sleep as well. Inadequate sleep has been linked to various negative mental health consequences, including daytime fatigue, difficulty concentrating, impaired cognitive function, mood disturbances, and an increased risk of accidents. Those problems are generally the first signs of poor sleep. If inadequate sleep continues, the risk of developing many health diseases such as obesity, diabetes, cardiovascular disease, and mental health disorders also increases. Without adequate sleep, the mind and body quickly fall apart.

Functions of Sleep

1. **Restoration and Rejuvenation:** While sleeping, the body undergoes restorative processes to begin healing itself from all the micro trauma from the day. Tissues and muscles are repaired, the body's energy system is replenished, and sleep helps support the immune system, promotes healing, and maintains optimal physical functioning.
   ◆ Your body repairs wounds, repairs muscle breakdown from hard workouts, recovers from sickness and illness, and prepares you for the next day's worth of activity while you sleep.
2. **Memory Consolidation:** While sleeping, your brain consolidates and organizes memories. It transfers all the information you learned from your short-term memory into your long-term memory, which is important for learning and retaining information throughout life.

Chapter 11: Introduction to Sleep (cont.)

◆ Think of your brain as a filing system. You have your short-term memory in one room and your long-term memory in another room. While you sleep, your brain works hard to take the important information from the day in your short-term memory and transport it into your long-term memory so you never forget the information. Without doing this, it would be impossible to remember information for tests.

3. **Cognitive Function and Performance:** Sufficient sleep is essential for optimal cognitive function, which includes attention, concentration, problem-solving, decision-making, creativity, motor learning, and critical thinking.

   ◆ If you've practiced free throws or a dancing routine, sleep is when your body remembers the modifications you made while practicing throughout that day so your body remembers how to do everything you've learned. If you have a hard time focusing, decision-making, or thinking outside the box, there's a high probability you're not getting enough sleep throughout the night.

4. **Emotional Regulation:** Sleep helps to stabilize your mood, improve emotional resilience, and reduce the risk of developing mood disorders such as anxiety and depression. Sleep regulates emotions and emotional processing.

   ◆ Without sleep, your "fuse" becomes shorter. This means you are more likely to act out or "burst" when you're upset. Sleep is how your brain learns to calm itself down and prevent outbursts when bad things happen. Unfortunately, bad things continue to happen throughout life so it is important to get adequate sleep so you can continue to respond appropriately to bad things instead of overreacting.

5. **Hormonal Regulation:** Sleep helps regulate many hormones in the body that influence appetite, metabolism, and energy regulation. Lack of sleep can disrupt hormonal balance and contribute to weight gain and metabolic imbalances and increase risk of conditions like diabetes and obesity.

   ◆ People who don't get very much sleep slow their metabolism down over time. They also make poorer eating decisions and are generally hungrier the following day. This makes it easier to gain unwanted body fat and harder to lose weight when dieting and exercising. When trying to get or maintain a healthy body weight, sleep is an absolute necessity.

6. **Physical Health and Disease Prevention:** Adequate sleep is associated with a reduced risk of cardiovascular disease, obesity, diabetes, and cancer. Sleep supports healthy immune function, reduces inflammation, and promotes increased overall physical well-being.

   ◆ If sleep is what recovers your body, not getting enough sleep never allows you to recover and just wears you down over time. If you drove your car nonstop for days, it would overheat and break down. Your body is no different—it needs rest to recover and protect itself from disease.

7. **Mental Health and Well-Being:** Sleep is closely linked to depression and anxiety. Lack of sleep significantly increases the risk for developing many mental health disorders and makes symptoms of already developed mental health disorders, such as ADHD or OCD, much worse.

   ◆ These changes happen very quickly in the short term, and it doesn't take long before weeks or months go by and wear down your mental health. Try to notice how you feel when you get one night of bad sleep. Typically you'll feel sadder and more anxious the entire next day. If you continue this cycle, you will continue to feel worse and worse.

Chapter 11: Introduction to Sleep (cont.)

Sleep Duration Needs by Age

Sleep needs actually vary by age. The body requires more rest when you are growing, meaning newborns, who grow incredibly fast, need the most amount of sleep, and the amount of sleep you need goes down as you stop growing. The younger you are, the more sleep you need to continue optimal growth and development. Typically, 8 hours of sleep is recommended universally, but the needs of school-aged children and teenagers actually are much higher than that.

1. **Newborns** (0–3 months): 14–17 hours of sleep per day, including daytime naps
2. **Infants** (4–11 months): 12–15 hours of sleep per day, including daytime naps
3. **Toddlers** (1–2 years): 11–14 hours of sleep per day, including a nap or two
4. **Preschoolers** (3–5 years): 10–13 hours of sleep per day, including a nap or quiet time
5. **School-age children** (6–13 years): 9–11 hours of sleep per day
6. **Teenagers** (14–17 years): 8–10 hours of sleep per day
7. **Adults** (18–64 years): 7–9 hours of sleep per day, although individual variations exist
8. **Older adults** (65 years and older): 7–8 hours of sleep per day

Let's pretend you are in high school and you need 10 hours of sleep. School starts at 8 A.M. and it takes you about an hour to get ready so you set your alarm for 7 A.M. What time do you have to go to sleep in order to get all 10 hours of sleep to feel your best? To do this, count backwards from 7 A.M. If you went to bed at midnight, that would give you 7 hours of sleep, but you still need 3 more hours. Subtract 3 from 12 and your "bedtime" would be 9 P.M. every night. If you have to get up even earlier to ride a bus to school, you will have to go to bed earlier.

Many teenagers do not get close to the amount of sleep they need per night, which is thought to be one reason why so many mental health disorders, such as anxiety and depression, are skyrocketing across this population.

Key Notes

- **Sleep** is a naturally recurring state of reduced consciousness and physical activity in which a person's body and mind rest and regenerate. It is an essential physiological process that allows the body to recover, repair tissues, form memories, and reset from a long day's worth of activity.
- **Functions of Sleep**
  - **Restoration and Rejuvenation**
  - **Memory Consolidation**
  - **Cognitive Function and Performance**
  - **Emotional Regulation**
  - **Hormonal Regulation**
  - **Physical Health and Disease Prevention**
  - **Mental Health and Well-Being**

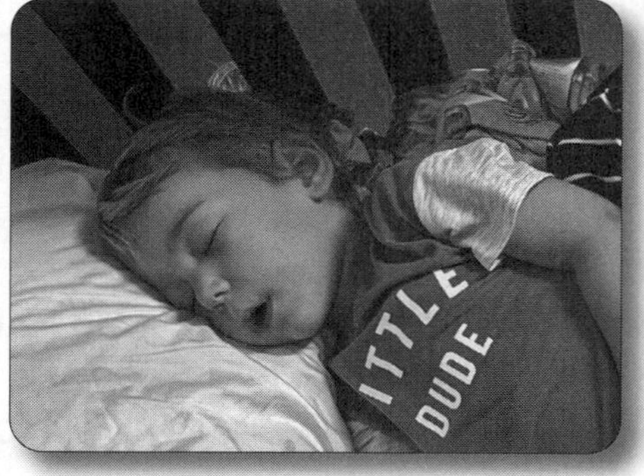

- **Sleep Duration Needs by Age**
  - **Newborns** (14–17 hours)
  - **Infants** (12–15 hours)
  - **Toddlers** (11–14 hours)
  - **Preschoolers** (10–13 hours)
  - **School-aged children** (9–11 hours)
  - **Teenagers** (8–10 hours)
  - **Adults** (7–9 hours)
  - **Older adults** (7–8 hours)

Chapter 11: Introduction to Sleep (cont.)

Activity: Sleep Tracker

Instructions for Students: Record your hours of consecutive, uninterrupted sleep for an entire week. After each night, record how you feel after waking up, at mid-day, and a summary of how you felt at the end of the day. You should notice how much better you feel, how your days are happier, and ultimately, how you are experiencing a higher quality of life when you're getting enough sleep. On the nights you don't get enough sleep, you will probably report the following day feeling drowsy, agitated, anxious, etc., and more so throughout the day.

It is important to understand that sleep has a direct impact on how you feel and how your mood is regulated. The better sleep you get, the happier you'll be when you're awake. By tracking your sleep and shining a light on the problem, it makes you aware that your sleep may be why you don't feel well and why you might not perform as well as you could in life and at school.

Day	Hours of Sleep	How I'm Feeling		
		Morning	**Mid-Day**	**End of Day**
Sun.				
Mon.				
Tue.				
Wed.				
Thur.				
Fri.				
Sat.				

Chapter 12: Sleep and Circadian Rhythm

Definition and Explanation of Circadian Rhythm

The National Institute of General Medical Sciences defines a **circadian rhythm** as a physical, mental, and behavioral change that follows a 24-hour cycle. This can be easily thought of as a **sleep-wake cycle**, which basically explains when and why you're awake and asleep throughout 24 hours of a day. Your body is born with a **biological clock**, referred to as your **suprachiasmatic nucleus** located in the hypothalamus, that takes in information from light and uses that information to release hormones that help regulate your sleep at night and your alertness during the day.

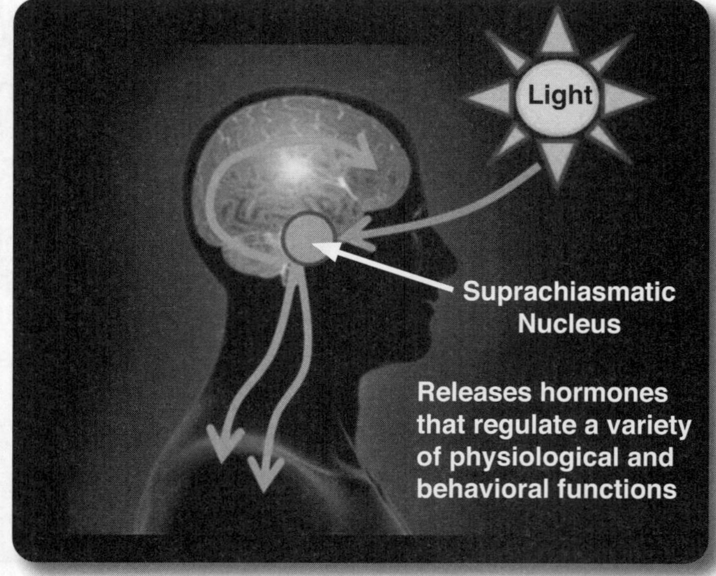

The circadian rhythm regulates sleep-wake cycles, hormone production, body temperature, metabolism, and alertness levels. Your body LOVES routine. It prefers to wake up and go to sleep at the same time every day. When it is in sync, it performs very well. When it's time to go to bed, your body releases a hormone called **melatonin**, which tells your body it's time for sleep. As morning approaches, melatonin decreases and your body becomes more alert, which is why you wake up. How does the body know when to release melatonin and when to stop producing melatonin so you wake up alert and stay alert throughout the day?

How Light Exposure Regulates the Circadian Clock

Melatonin is regulated by light exposure. When it's dark or the room is dim, your eyes don't take in as much light. This tells your pineal gland to release higher amounts of melatonin, which signals to the body to prepare for sleep and promotes drowsiness. When the lights are bright, the eyes detect more light and decrease the amount of melatonin in the brain, which promotes wakefulness and alertness during the day.

This is why it's so hard to wake up in the winter when it's still dark outside in the morning and why you get tired much more quickly when the days are shorter in the midst of winter. Your body is getting much less sunlight, which makes you drowsier. In the summer, it seems like most people have an abundance of energy because the days are longer. When the sun pokes through the blinds of the windows, your eyes still get signals of light even though they are closed. This helps prompt the body to wake up and helps regulate your sleep cycle. If you get bright, natural, sunlight first thing in the morning, it sets up your entire day to be alert and awake. By avoiding light before bed, your body begins to produce more melatonin, which helps you fall asleep faster and stay asleep.

Sleep-Wake Cycles

A **sleep-wake cycle** refers to the 24-hour day in which our bodies alternate between sleep and wakefulness. While the external environment, such as light, helps regulate this process with the use of melatonin, it is also important to note that genetically the body has its own internal biological clock. Some people, often referred to as night owls, actually perform better at night,

Chapter 12: Sleep and Circadian Rhythm (cont.)

maintaining higher focus, alertness, and creativity during the night hours. While this is genetic, it is important to note that your body still PREFERS to fall asleep and wake up at the same time every day and still REQUIRES a certain amount of sleep to perform well. So even if you are a night owl, if you have a daytime job or go to school in the morning, you still need to maintain a normal sleeping schedule to ensure you get enough rest to recover.

You can use sunlight to adjust your sleep-wake cycle. Your body is incredibly resilient and can change very well when your day-to-day demands are different. So even if you're a night owl, at least during the school year, you will have to take extra care to maintain a healthy sleep hygiene in order to perform well. Once you're an adult, your genetic makeup may mean you will do better working at a job on the second or third shift during the night.

Factors Affecting Sleepiness and Alertness Throughout the Day

There are many factors that influence sleepiness and alertness throughout the day. Understanding these factors can help you develop your own sleep routine and perform your best during school, work, or physical activity. Remember, your body loves routine and would prefer to go to sleep and wake up at the same time every day, so this is the number one factor that affects your sleepiness and alertness. Others include:

1. **Circadian Rhythm:** the body's internal clock that, once in sync, prefers to wake up and go to sleep at the same time every day. This is why it's important to wake up at the same time, even on the weekends, throughout the week. If you sleep in on the weekend, that throws off your entire circadian rhythm for days after. This makes it very hard to wake up early on Monday and Tuesday, throwing off half of your week.

2. **Light Exposure:** Primarily natural sunlight helps promote alertness. It is recommended to get natural sunlight for at least 10 minutes first thing in the morning. During the summer months, go sit outside and look near the sunrise. This will promote wakefulness and start up your day. If the sun is not out, turn on the lights in your room as bright as they can go. While nothing beats real sunlight, any bright light will help promote wakefulness and help regulate your circadian rhythm. Before bed, dim the lights and reduce the amount of light your eyes are getting. DO NOT look at electronics or TVs, as these blue lights tell your brain to stay up. This is why it's so hard to fall asleep when checking your phone throughout the night.

3. **Sleep Duration and Quality:** The amount of sleep you got the night before significantly impacts how you feel the following day. If you didn't get enough sleep, you will fight excessive daytime sleepiness all day, which often can feel like symptoms of depression. If you get enough restorative rest, that will promote daytime alertness, making it easier to focus and study all day long.

4. **Time Awake:** The longer you've been awake, the more the need for sleep builds up. When you have to stay up later than intended for different events or projects, it is normal for your body to get drowsy after being awake for a long time.

5. **Physical Activity:** Regular physical activity increases alertness. Exercise releases neurotransmitters and hormones that promote wakefulness and improve alertness. If you are someone who struggles with waking yourself up in the morning, morning exercise does a great job to wake you up all day long. If you are someone who finds themselves getting drowsy in the middle of the day, you can time your workouts for lunch and promote more alertness and focus during the second half of your day.

Chapter 12: Sleep and Circadian Rhythm (cont.)

6. **Nutrition and Hydration:** Because neurotransmitters and hormones require protein and fat to build and energy requires carbohydrates, it is crucial to consume a balanced diet throughout the day to help sustain alertness. Dehydration can also make you tired, so stay on top of your water intake as well. Start your morning off with a glass of water to help ensure you stay hydrated.

7. **Caffeine and Stimulants:** Caffeinated beverages can provide short boosts in alertness. Because your body gets used to caffeine so quickly, it is recommended to use caffeine sparingly on an as-needed basis. Proper sleep hygiene, physical activity, light activity, and eating a balanced diet will do more for your alertness than caffeine ever will. Consuming caffeine too close to bedtime can also disrupt and impair sleep, making you more tired the following day.

8. **Medications:** Some medications can promote sedative qualities and make you more tired throughout the day. Make sure to review the side effects of any medications you're taking. Many will come with a warning not to drive or operate heavy machinery if they promote drowsiness.

9. **Individual Differences:** Individual differences such as age, genetics, stress, and other health conditions can influence an individual's baseline level of sleepiness and alertness as well.

Consequences of Poor Sleep

Sleep regulates so many different biological factors within our bodies, it is no wonder it is referred to as the Third Pillar of Health. We've previously discussed many of the consequences of poor sleep, but it is crucial to have these consequences listed and remembered to really drive home just how important it is to get adequate sleep, especially while you're young.

1. **Daytime Sleepiness/Fatigue:** Poor sleep can lead to increased fatigue throughout the day, reduced alertness, difficulty concentrating, reduced productivity, and an increase in mistakes and errors.
    ◆ This can have a direct impact on your school and work, making it harder to think in class and making it harder to remember answers and problem-solve. It can also hurt your physical performance during sports, learning new plays and movements.

2. **Impaired Cognitive Function:** Sleep regulates and maintains cognitive functions such as memory, attention, problem-solving, and decision-making. Lack of sleep impairs all of these functions and decreases mental clarity, decreases memory recall (remembering things), reduces creativity, and creates difficulties in learning and retaining information.
    ◆ Poor sleep makes it harder to create art, learn algebra, write papers, and remember multiple-choice questions, all worsening your grades at school. When working, this will also decrease your performance as well, making it harder to get promoted and get raises.

Chapter 12: Sleep and Circadian Rhythm (cont.)

3. **Mood Disturbances:** Inadequate sleep is associated with irritability, mood swings, increased stress levels, and increasing the risk for depression and anxiety disorders.
   - Being in a positive mood and having a positive outlook on life will improve your life in many different ways. Making sure to get enough sleep is the first step to improving your mental health.

4. **Weakened Immune Function:** Sleep plays a critical role in supporting your immune system. Chronic sleep deprivation weakens the immune system.
   - A weak immune system makes you more likely to get sick, get infections, recover more slowly from illness, and repair wounds and injuries more slowly. Chronic sleep deprivation can lead to major diseases such as cardiovascular disease, diabetes, and obesity as well.

5. **Impaired Physical Health:** Poor sleep causes changes in your hormones and neurotransmitters. These changes can disrupt appetite-regulating hormones and lead to overeating and weight gain. Poor sleep impairs your coordination and recovery from sports and exercise, making you weaker and worse at the things you enjoy doing.
   - Exercisers and athletes especially need sleep to recover from strenuous workouts and make continual improvements to their health.

6. **Increased Pain Sensitivity:** Poor sleep also increases the amount of pain you feel throughout the day. If you suffer from low back pain, neck pain, knee pain—any sort of pain—your brain perceives it as being more painful than it actually is when you don't get enough sleep.
   - Sleep should be your first priority when recovering from any injury, which includes chronic aches and pains.

7. **Impaired Social and Interpersonal Functioning:** Poor sleep can increase irritability, decrease empathy, and lead to poorer communication, all things that allow you to relate and befriend other people and work together in groups.
   - Humans are designed to work well in groups and be social. This is how we have managed to stay alive as a species for so long. Poor sleep makes it harder to connect with people and loved ones in general. Connectedness decreases depression and anxiety and also helps ensure a successful life, since knowing and befriending people opens up so many more doors in life. Sleep is crucial for maintaining healthy relationships.

As you can see, there are many consequences of sleep deprivation and getting poor sleep. One night of poor sleep is not likely to wreck your health, but it is a slippery slope with sleep. One night often turns into two nights, which ends up being weeks or months. It is crucial that even when one night of sleep is disrupted, you maintain your healthy sleeping habits the following night so that you don't fall into a pattern of poor sleep, which will likely lead to many of these poor health consequences.

Chapter 12: Sleep and Circadian Rhythm (cont.)

Key Notes
- **Definition and Explanation of Circadian Rhythm**
- **How Light Exposure Regulates the Circadian Clock**
  - **Melatonin**
- **Sleep-Wake Cycles**
- **Factors Affecting Sleepiness and Alertness Throughout the Day**
  - **Circadian Rhythm**
  - **Light Exposure**
  - **Sleep Duration and Quality**
  - **Time Awake**
  - **Physical Activity**
  - **Nutrition and Hydration**
  - **Caffeine and Stimulants**
  - **Medications**
  - **Individual Differences**
- **Consequences of Poor Sleep**
  - **Daytime Sleepiness/Fatigue**
  - **Impaired Cognitive Function**
  - **Mood Disturbances**
  - **Weakened Immune Function**
  - **Impaired Physical Health**
  - **Increased Pain Sensitivity**
  - **Impaired Social and Interpersonal Functioning**

Activity: How Does Light Affect Your Ability to Fall Asleep?

Instructions for Teachers: This activity is designed to help kids understand how different levels of light influence alertness and drowsiness and put them in better/worse positions to fall asleep. Have students spend 10 minutes in natural light (preferably outdoors) where they can choose to journal, create art, or read. Then they mark where they are on the "drowsy to alert" scale with natural light. Next, students are brought inside into bright artificial light where they are asked to do the same, followed by self-reporting on the drowsy to alert scale. Next, shut the blinds or cover the windows and only offer a dim artificial light in the classroom. Students can continue to journal, read, or create art, but they must keep their eyes open. Again, they mark where they are on the drowsy to alert scale. Finally, shut off the lights and cover windows completely. Try to tape over any LED or other artificial light in the room. Ask the students to try to keep their eyes open, even though it's dark. They can continue to try to journal or create art if they'd like, just without light. Have them rate their drowsy to alertness. By the end of the activity, students should see a clear line shifting toward drowsiness to eventually fighting the urge to fall asleep altogether. This shows students the importance of setting the mood for sleep, beginning to dim the lights, finding relaxing activities before bed, and eliminating any lights throughout the room from electronics.

Drowsy   **Alert**
10—9—8—7—6—5—4—3—2—1—0—1—2—3—4—5—6—7—8—9—10

Try to make sure kids don't have any caffeine up to 4 hours previous to the activity for best results.

Chapter 13: Building Up Sleep Hygiene

Sleep hygiene refers to the habits and practices that promote healthy, restful sleep. As previously mentioned, by understanding the mechanisms of the sleep-wake cycle, like light, we can build healthy habits (sleep hygiene) in order to ensure that our circadian rhythm stays in sync every day, which will promote all the benefits of regeneration and rejuvenation of sleep. Sleep hygiene thrives on adopting behaviors and creating environments that will help support and maintain optimal sleep quality and quantity.

Establish a Regular Sleep Schedule

Figuring out your sleep schedule based on your lifestyle is the first step in creating healthy sleep hygiene. Through a series of steps previously discussed throughout this book, we can build our own sleep schedule based on our individual needs.

1. **Determine your sleep needs:** Based on the chart in Chapter 11, identify how many hours of rest per night you need. Most adults and teenagers require between 7–10 hours of sleep per night. Refer to your sleep tracker journal in Chapter 11 where you recorded how many hours of sleep you got and how you felt throughout the day. If you feel great getting 9 hours of sleep but drowsy with 8 hours or 10 hours, you know that 9 hours is your ideal sleep time for you.

2. **Establish a wake-up time:** Because we all have responsibilities such as school, work, or athletics we have to wake up for, identify when you have to get up throughout the week. You must use your EARLIEST wake up time as your wake-up time throughout the week to ensure a consistent schedule. That means if you have to wake up by 7 A.M. to get to school by 8 A.M. during the week, then  on the weekend, even though you don't have to wake up for school, you should still wake up at 7 A.M. to maintain your rhythm and stay in sync with your cycle. Because wake-up time is usually dictated by responsibilities outside of your control, it is the second component to building a good sleep routine.

3. **Set a consistent bedtime:** Now that you know how many hours of sleep you need per night and you know when you have to wake up for school or work, you can then work backwards to figure out when you have to go to bed. If you have to wake up by 6 A.M. to get ready for the day and you require 10 hours of sleep to feel your best, work 10 hours back from 6 A.M., and you will have an optimal bedtime of around 8 P.M. Generally, if it takes you 10–15 minutes to fall asleep, you would want to get in bed closer to 7:45 to ensure the 10 hours. This should be your fixed bedtime, even during the weekend. Try to come as close to this schedule as possible. Even if you have to stay up later than intended, still wake up at the same time. It is better to feel off for one day rather than throw your entire week off schedule by sleeping in and throwing off your next day as well.

4. **Adjust slowly:** If your schedule suddenly changes, it is best to adjust your sleep schedule in 30-minute increments over a series of days to avoid disrupting your entire cycle. Daylight Saving Time is a good example of throwing off your entire week. It takes some people several weeks to feel normal after just adjusting their schedule one hour forward or back.

Practical Tips for Building a Sleep Routine

Because the body craves stability and routine, building a relaxing routine around bedtime helps signal to the body it is time to unwind and fall asleep. Doing the same thing before bed every night helps make it much easier to fall asleep because you're setting your brain up for the habit.

Chapter 13: Building Up Sleep Hygiene (cont.)

Dedicate 30–60 minutes before bed to your sleep routine. Some tips and examples can include the following:

1. **Put your electronics on the charger 60 minutes prior to bed to ensure you don't check them before bed.** The blue light signals to your brain to stay awake, which is the opposite of what you're trying to do when you're building a good sleep routine. This includes your cell phone, TV, tablet, and LED lights within the room.
2. **Take a warm bath or shower.** Warm water helps relax the muscles and promotes a feeling of relaxation. Showering before bed can also save you a lot of time in the morning and allow you to sleep in later.
3. **Practice dental and skincare hygiene.** Prior to bed, brush your teeth and follow your regular skincare routine, which usually includes moisturizer before bed. This will keep your teeth and skin healthy, and also promotes relaxation and prepares you for bed.
4. **Keep a book next to your bed and read it before bed.** Books, unlike electronics, have a relaxing effect and help you unwind for the day. Be careful to choose books that aren't too stimulating, as scary books or other thriller books might keep you up at night.
5. **Dim the lights in your room while you read and prepare for bed.** Remember, melatonin production is triggered by the lack of light. By dimming the lights, you're stimulating more melatonin production, which will help you fall asleep faster.

These are just a few examples of ways to build your bedtime routine. The most important thing is to do the same things every time before bed. These will trigger your body to fall asleep and help you keep your circadian rhythm. If you're someone who has a hard time falling asleep, building a routine may help immensely. Things can always be added to or subtracted from your routine based on your individual needs and differences.

Creating a Comfortable Sleeping Environment

Your sleeping environment is just as important as your routine for getting to sleep and staying asleep. If you don't feel comfortable or safe in your environment, it will be very hard to get restful, quality sleep at night. There are many tricks and tips to ensure a healthy sleeping environment, such as:

1. **Keeping your room cool.** While there is no set optimal temperature, most people do well with cooler rooms at night. You can experiment with temperatures and fans to find what is most comfortable for you.
2. **Keep your room as dark as possible.** Try not to let light from outside poke through your room or stay in your field of vision while you're asleep. While opening your blinds first thing in the morning will help you wake up, the last thing you want before bed is any light keeping you up. This includes LED lights in your room coming from computers, gaming systems, or other electronics. Tape over these lights to help make sure they don't bother you when trying to go to sleep. If you can't eliminate all light, consider using an eye mask.
3. **Block out as much noise as you can.** Using white noise machines or fans is a great way to create a soothing ambient sound that blocks out outside noise factors such as trains, cars,

Chapter 13: Building Up Sleep Hygiene (cont.)

and even creaks within your own home. Consider using ear plugs if the outside sound is keeping you up.

4. **Comfortable beds, pillows, and sheets will also help you feel comfortable and ensure quality sleep.** As bedding technology has grown over the last decade, you may have to experiment with different firmness levels of pillows and beds to find with which you fall asleep the easiest.

5. **Keep your room clean and free from chaos.** When your room is messy, you're living in a constant state of chaos. Even if you don't mind the mess, often times this environment will make it harder to fall asleep, knowing you should clean your room. By keeping it tidy, you keep your sleeping environment clean, and it relaxes you since you don't find things you need to clean before bed.

6. **Put your phone and other electronics on "do not disturb."** Remember, the light will impair your ability to fall asleep. By putting your phone on "do not disturb," you won't get notifications and be tempted to check your phone throughout the night.

These are just some tips and strategies to account for when building up your sleeping environment. There are so many individual differences when it comes to what is considered a comfortable sleeping environment. Experiment on your own to find out what your body responds to best.

Creating a Wake-Up Routine

Creating a wake-up routine is the last and final component to establishing and maintaining a healthy sleep-wake cycle. Just as a sleep routine helps your brain relax and prepare for rest, a good wake-up routine will help increase alertness, set up your day for success, and prevent you from being tired, groggy, and irritable in the morning. Here are some tips to building a solid wake-up routine:

1. **Set a consistent wake-up time every day.** Like we previously noted, it is important to wake up at the same time every day, even on the weekends. This helps regulate your body's internal clock and keeps a consistent sleep-wake cycle.

2. **Use an alarm clock across the room.** Many people use their phone's alarm clock and sleep next to it. It can be very easy to hit snooze in the mornings and fall back asleep. By getting an alarm clock and keeping it across the room, you force yourself to wake up, get out of bed, walk across the room, and shut the alarm clock off. These extra steps will make it much harder to fall back asleep.

3. **Open your blinds or find other natural light as soon as you are up.** Exposure to natural light signals to slow down melatonin production, which increases alertness and tells your body it's time to wake up and start the day. If you don't have access to natural light, turn on the lights in the house.

4. **Get your body moving with an easy, active routine.** Do some pushups or some air squats to get your blood pumping and release neurotransmitters that wake up your body. A brief 2-minute bout of exercise is enough to wake you up.

5. **Drink a glass of water as soon as you wake up.** You likely haven't had any hydration all night long. Getting water into your body will help kickstart your metabolism and help you stay hydrated in the morning.

Chapter 13: Building Up Sleep Hygiene (cont.)

6. **Eat a nutritious breakfast.** Even if you make your breakfast the day before and reheat it, try to eat something first thing in the morning, as this energy will help you in all you are required to do for the day. Make sure to include healthy protein, complex carbohydrates, and vegetables or fruit.

7. **Brush your teeth and prepare for the day.** End your morning routine with taking care of your personal hygiene such as teeth brushing and applying deodorant, followed by getting dressed and ready for school or work. By this time, you should be awake and prepared for the day ahead.

Exactly the same as your sleep routine, your wake-up routine will set the entire tone for the day. It is important to try and follow this routine even on the weekends to ensure you don't fall out of the habit. Plan events or things to do on the weekends in the morning. That way you have a reason and a purpose to get out of the door in the morning. Without purpose, it is very difficult to force yourself out of bed. Finding meaningful things to do on the weekend will help you keep and maintain a great quality of life and stay on top of your sleep-wake cycle.

Key Notes
- **Sleep hygiene** refers to the habits and practices that promote healthy, restful sleep.
- **Establish a Regular Sleep Schedule**
  - **Determine your sleep needs**
  - **Establish a wake-up time**
  - **Set a consistent bedtime**
  - **Adjust slowly**
- **Practical Tips for Building a Sleep Routine**
  - **Put up electronics 60 minutes before bed**
  - **Take a warm bath or shower**
  - **Practice dental/skincare hygiene**
  - **Keep a book next to your bed to read**
  - **Dim the lights before bed**

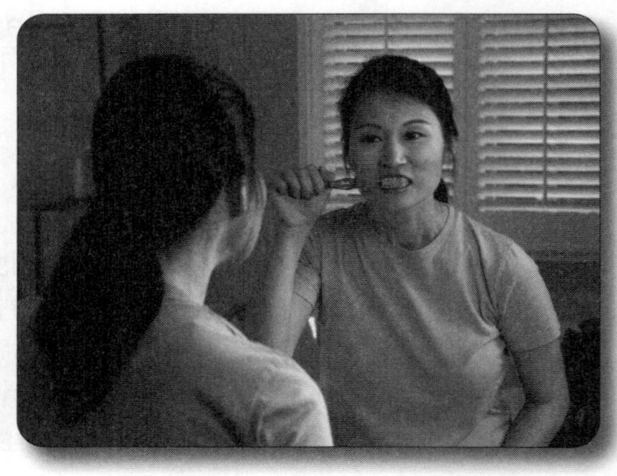

- **Creating a Comfortable Sleeping Environment**
  - **Keep your room cool**
  - **Keep your room as dark as possible**
  - **Block out noise/use white noise**
  - **Comfortable bed/pillow/sheets**
  - **Keep your room clean**
  - **Put electronics on "do not disturb"**
- **Creating a Wake-Up Routine**
  - **Set a consistent wake-up time every day**
  - **Use an alarm clock across the room**
  - **Get natural light as soon as possible when you get up**
  - **Get your body moving with an easy, active routine**
  - **Drink water immediately**
  - **Eat a nutritious breakfast**
  - **Brush your teeth and prepare for the day**

Chapter 13: Building Up Sleep Hygiene (cont.)

Activity: Building Your Bedtime Routine

Instructions for Students: Build your ideal bedtime routine, whether that's brushing your teeth, reading a book, talking with your parents about the day, etc. List out your ideal ways of relaxing and unwinding for the day. After listing your perfect bedtime routine, try it for one week and record how many hours of sleep you got as well as how easy it was to go to sleep versus the previous week. Ideally, you will be able to go to sleep much easier after the routine, and your sleep should be much more restful. After noting how much better you sleep, you can hopefully continue these habits down the road. Be sure to shut off cell phone/electronics 60 minutes before bedtime.

Activity: Building Your Morning Routine

Instructions for Students: After the bedtime routine is established, use the tips and tricks taking advantage of movement and light to build your morning routine. Write down what you feel would make for the perfect morning routine to wake up and get excited about the day, whether that's listening to some upbeat music in the shower or doing a morning micro workout. Try this routine before school for one week, noting your energy levels throughout the day. Hopefully by this time, you will feel much better after having established your bedtime routine and taking advantage of the tips and tricks to start your mornings off better. It takes some time for habits to form, so try to continue using your routines beyond the class assignments.

A tidy bedroom can be a more relaxing environment than a messy bedroom.

Healthy Eating, Exercise, and Sleep Photo Credits

Unless otherwise noted, photo images were found on Wikimedia Commons <https://commons.wikimedia.org/wiki/> at the file name listed.

Front Cover:

Laughing preteen kids posing with sport equipment {©istockphoto.com} LightFieldStudios. 23 May 2019. Stock photo ID: 1151201944.

Getting Stronger {©istockphoto.com} dberol. 13 Apr 2012. Stock photo ID: 177023184.

Teenage girls enjoy eating breakfast before go to school, Back to school concept {©istockphoto.com} Danai Jetawattana. 20 Jul 2022. Stock photo ID: 1409303953.

African American little girl doing meditate yoga asana with eyes closed outdoor in park. Kids girl practicing doing yoga outdoor. {©istockphoto.com} Amorn Suriyan. 12 Sept 2021. Stock photo ID: 1339647971.

Happy young female runner winning on race finish {©istockphoto.com} dolgachov. 21 Oct 2015. Stock photo ID: 492221120.

Chef teacher teaches cooking to the group children in class kitchen room. Chef preparing student for learning marking and cooking food at workshop. Education Concept {©istockphoto.com} Wand_Prapan. 21 Feb 2023. Stock photo ID: 1461342115.

Happy African American schoolboy stretching during PE class at school gym. {©istockphoto.com} Drazen Zigic. 17 Aug 2021. Stock photo ID: 1334046768.

A young man with white hair is sleeping in his bed. {©istockphoto.com} Hanna Shyriaieva. 11 Jan 2022. Stock photo ID: 1361745993.

pg. iv   Healthy food ingredients.jpg {CC BY-DA 4.0} Dan Gold. 19 Mar 2021. Mercymuchai7. 19 Mar 2021.

pg. iv   Learning How to Use Weights {©istockphoto.com} FatCamera. 25 Nov 2015. Stock photo ID: 498579050.

pg. 1   The SugarBee Apple now grown in Washington State.jpg {CC BY-SA 4.0} DinMutha. 23 Dec 2014. User-duck. 9 Sept 2022.

pg. 1   Patisserie Norina Truffle Torte Cake Slice (23034176760).jpg {CC BY-SA 2.0} Willis Lam. 3 May 2015. Ser Amantio di Nicolao. 5 May 2019.

pg. 2   Protein-rich Foods.jpg {CC BY-SA 4.0} Smastronardo. 18. Oct 2014.

pg. 2   Foods (cropped).jpg {PD-USGov, USDA} Keith Weller, Agricultural Research Service, USDA. 14 Mar 2013. Northamerica1000. 14 Mar 2013.

pg. 3   Foods with a high fibre content, such as bread, grains, chia seeds and nuts.jpg {CC BY 2.0} formulatehealth. 23 Sept 2020. Formulatehealth. 28 Nov 2020.

pg. 3   Butter and Knive.jpg {PD-Author, CC0 1.0} Julikalucky. 23 Jun 2023. Julikalucky. 29 Jun 2023.

pg. 4   Olive Oil (50316477903).jpg {CC BY 2.0} ajay_suresh. 29 Aug 2020. Epicsunwarrior. 31 May 2021.

pg. 4   Healthy Deit For A Healthy Well Well and Leave.jpg {CC BY-SA 4.0} Ceciliaakan. 18 Mar 2021.

pg. 6   Chicken breast on Vegetables - 49859595051.jpg {CC BY-SA 2.0} FitTasteTic. 26 Oct 2019. Ser Amantio di Nicolao. 25 Nov 2020.

pg. 6   Pizza (27551169537).jpg {CC BY 2.0} Dale Cruse from San Francisco, CA, USA. 26 Apr 2018. Netha Hussain. 11 Oct 2019.

pg. 8   Սաղմոնի ուտեստ.JPG (Baked salmon, wedged potatoes, asparagus and zucchini, with mac and cheese) {CC BY-SA 3.0} Chaojoker. 18 Dec 2011. Chaojoker. 31 Jan 2012.

pg. 9   2019-07-20 13 27 43 A mushroom cheeseburger and french fries at Texas Tradition in Katy, Harris County, Texas.jpg {CC BY-SA 4.0} Famartin. 20 Jul 2019. Famartin. 22 Jul 2019.

pg. 9   Salad with strawberries.jpg {CC BY-SA 3.0} Little-Known-Food-Facts. 21 Oct 2007.

pg. 10   Food Label.png {CC BY-SA 4.0} BruceBlaus. 6 Apr 2017.

pg. 12   Tracking calories burned cycling.jpg {CC BY-SA 4.0} Alextredz. 27 Jul 2021. Alextredz. 28 Jul 2021.

pg. 13   Amity Spartan player jumping for the ball.jpg {CC BY-SA 4.0} JamesReynolds331. 9 Sept 2022. JamesReynolds331. 5 Dec 2022.

pg. 13   Football game 1.jpg {CC BY-SA 4.0} Julianechavarr44. 30 Aug 2021.

pg. 13   Eating a 'bhutta'.jpg {CC BY-SA 4.0} Gopi Sutar. 13 Jun 2015.

pg. 14   Participation in sport - Lefelau cyfranogiad mewn chwaraeon (13129670834).jpg {CC BY 2.0} National Assembly for Wales from Wales. 13 Mar 2014. Tm. 11 Aug 2016.

pg. 15   KC Ballet IMG 5246 (16475601720).jpg {CC BY 2.0} KCBalletMedia. 26 Feb 2015. Elisfkc. 5 Mar 2016.

pg. 15   ESPN Zone Chicago Ultimate Couch Potato Contestant - Steve Janowski 03.JPG {PD-Author} LAIntern at en.wikipedia. 28 Mar 2009. BotMultichill. 6 May 2009.

pg. 17   Blausen 0012 AdiposeTissue.png {CC BY 3.0} BruceBlaus. Blausen.com staff (2014). "Medical gallery of Blausen Medical 2014." *WikiJournal of Medicine 1 (2)*. DOI:10.15347/wjm/2014.010. ISSN 2002-4436. 30 Sept 2013.

pg. 19   Step Count.jpg {CC BY-SA 4.0} U3177230. 17 Sept 2020.

pg. 22   20111019-FNS-RBN-1590 - Flickr - USDAgov.jpg {PD-USGov, USDA} Bob Nichols, USDA. 19 Oct 2011. BotMultichillT. 25 Dec 2011.

pg. 23   Culinary fruits front view.jpg {CC BY 3.0} Bill Ebbesen. 8 May 2010. Ionutzmovie. 13 Nov 2010.

pg. 24   A selection of vegetables 02.jpg {CC BY-SA 4.0} Rene Cortin. 22 Jun 2017. Green lama. 3 Oct 2017.

pg. 24   Bread and grains.jpg {PD-USGov, HHS} National Cancer Institute, National Institutes of Health, United States Department of Health and Human Services. Feb 1989. Fæ. 21 Jan 2013.

pg. 25   Protein (1).jpg {PD-USGov, HHS} National Cancer Institute, National Institutes of Health, United States Department of Health and Human Services. Mar 1989. Fæ. 21 Jan 2013.

pg. 26   Різні види молочних продуктів українського виробництва.jpg (Ukrainian dairy products) {PD-Author} Віктор Ходєєв. 2016. Modekolas. 6 Feb 2016.

pg. 26   Vegan Sausages, vegan coffee latte and a vegan muffin (5090679024).jpg {CC BY 2.0} Suzette - www.suzette.nu from Arnhem, Netherlands. 17 Oct 2010. John Cummings. 28 Sept 2014.

pg. 27   201110119-FNS-RBN-1646 - Flickr - USDAgov.jpg {PD-USGov, USDA} Bob Nichols, USDA. 19 Oct 2011. BotMultichillT. 25 Dec 2011.

pg. 28   File by Alexander Baranov - (14912393280).jpg {CC BY 2.0} Alexander Baranov from Montpellier, France. 16 Apr 2014. Sturm. 17 Nov 2015.

pg. 29   Breakfast in hotel 3.jpg {CC BY-SA 3.0} Tiia Monto. 30 Aug 2019. Kulmalukko. 1 Sept 2019.